T0295808

Emerging Technologies and the Indian IT Sector

This book examines the implementation of emerging technology projects in the service-based Indian IT sector. The title shows how emerging technologies impact IT-enabeled Services (ITeS) organizations and examines the mobility prospects for engineers and students looking to enter the Indian IT sector. Indian IT, dominated by organizations offering ITeS, provides services to clients across the world. Fueling this sector's growth are engineering graduates. Emerging technologies, such as AI, Big Data, Cloud, and Blockchain, have brought the IT and engineering education sectors to a crossroads with global implications. The IT sector is facing growing demands for new technology solutions from its clients, and it is engineering students who are expected to upskill in order to build these solutions. The volume provides a rare, bottom-up look at the intersection of technology, education, and organizational structure, based on an ethnographic study.

Emerging Technologies and the Indian IT Sector is a helpful and unique resource for managers in ITeS grappling with emerging technologies, researchers looking at how emerging technologies impact organizations, and those developing innovative IT courses in higher education. Readers interested in the global structure of IT education and industry will also find a fresh, ethnographically informed take on these issues.

Emerging Technologies and the Indian IT Sector

Vinay Reddy Venumuddala
and Rajalaxmi Kamath

CRC Press
Taylor & Francis Group
Boca Raton London New York

CRC Press is an imprint of the
Taylor & Francis Group, an **informa** business

A CHAPMAN & HALL BOOK

Designed cover image: Getty

[Seventh] edition published [2023]
by CRC Press
6000 Broken Sound Parkway NW, Suite 300, Boca Raton,
FL 33487-2742

and by CRC Press
4 Park Square, Milton Park, Abingdon, Oxon, OX14 4RN

CRC Press is an imprint of Taylor & Francis Group, LLC

© 2023 [Vinay Reddy Venumuddala and Rajalaxmi Kamath]

[First edition published by Willan 2008]
[Sixth edition published by Routledge 2009]

ISBN: 978-1-032-34900-8 (hbk)
ISBN: 978-1-032-34901-5 (pbk)
ISBN: 978-1-003-32435-5 (ebk)

DOI: 10.1201/9781003324355

Typeset in Bembo
by KnowledgeWorks Global Ltd.

Contents

Authors

Vinay Reddy Venumuddala completed his PhD in Public Policy area, at the Indian Institute of Management Bangalore (IIMB). His research interests lie at the intersection of Information Systems, Public Policy, and Electrical and Electronics Engineering. Presently, he is working as a post-doctoral fellow at the Centre for Internet of Ethical Things, International Institute of Information Technology, Bangalore.

Rajalaxmi Kamath is a professor at the Center for Public Policy at the Indian Institute of Management Bangalore (IIMB). Her research is around issues facing the development of the Indian economy, post 2000 – microfinance, and changing work conditions, with a very specific field-oriented, grounds-up approach to understanding them.

1 Introduction

1.1 The Indian IT industry and transition to emerging technologies

The Indian Information Technology (IT) industry in the city of Bengaluru, India, and the engineers working in it form the cornerstone of this book. This industry has grown in leaps and bounds through providing IT and IT-enabled services such as business process management (BPM) to clients across industry verticals around the globe. The IT-BPM services offered by this industry contribute to over 9% of the Indian GDP and claim close to 38% share in the total services exports of the country[1]. In terms of delivering such services to global clients, the established Indian IT services organizations achieved some of the highest process maturity levels and positioned themselves as highly reliable service providers[2]. The Indian IT services industry is also the largest private sector employer in the country with over 3.7 million jobs[3]. Software jobs in the IT services organizations have become aspirational for all types of engineers, and the city of Bengaluru, the IT capital of the country, has been a magnet attracting this talent. The availability of a large pool of engineers graduating every year from the engineering colleges across the country has been a key driving force for the growth of this industry[4]. The standardized work processes in these organizations meant that engineers, irrespective of their engineering backgrounds, could be molded into generic programmers capable of quickly adjusting to the rapidly evolving technologies and tools within the software industry[5]. Such a large workforce, available on-tap, also signaled the capabilities of these organizations to their long-standing clients[6].

In this book, we try and capture the ongoing transformation in this sector, where it finds itself riding the unceasing wave of digitization. Business clients of IT organizations across industry verticals are digitally transforming their businesses to remain sustainable in an increasingly competitive environment. As they seek to retain their customers, strategies to unleash the new industrial revolution – the 'industry 4.0' are becoming vital. Such strategies, fueled by emerging technologies, such as Artificial Intelligence (AI), Internet of Things (IoT), Blockchain, etc., are targeted toward making their processes more flexible and responsive toward the rapidly changing preferences

DOI: 10.1201/9781003324355-1

of their customers[7]. To fulfill their digital transformation objectives, many long-standing clients of the Indian IT services organizations are already outsourcing emerging-technology-based process improvement solutions to the latter[8]. Sensing opportunity to go further up the value chain, the Indian IT services organizations are making quick transitions by garnering expertise around AI, Cloud, IoT, Blockchain, etc. Many have already established in-house centers of excellence, or research labs, around emerging technologies to offer customized digital transformation solutions to clients[9]. One such AI research lab in a multinational IT organization in Bengaluru is our research site, providing us the vantage point for studying the developments in this sector.

We believe that the Indian IT services organizations are in a crucial transition phase in terms of witnessing an increasing demand for emerging technology-based digital transformation solutions from their clients. To understand the nature of this transition and the possible challenges faced by these organizations, the emerging technology research labs are key sites. This prompted our work ethnography in the said AI research lab in one such IT services organizations, which we refer to as ITSO. We discuss the background of this research context and details about our ethnography in Chapter 2. In this chapter, we provide a brief overview of our study's main objectives and also our findings. But, before going there, below, we elaborate on the transition of the Indian IT services organizations into the emerging technology space and introduce the importance of engineers in this context.

1.1.1 Transition to emerging technologies

The Indian IT services industry sustained during its initial growth period by providing services at the lower end of the value chain, taking advantage of the labor and cost arbitrage benefits that they provided to clients. It mainly offered software maintenance and business process outsourcing services. Over time, this industry came to be known for delivering high-quality services following mature process workflows, leading to a movement up the value chain in the software and BPM segments. The Indian IT services companies are now providing advanced services such as customized application development, customization of third-party enterprise applications, and so on to their clients[10]. In their current transition toward emerging technologies, the opportunities these companies seeing are around the augmentation of their traditional IT-BPM services through technologies like AI and Cloud. In the context of Cloud, they are offering modernization services to clients for revamping their legacy software systems into Cloud compatible software systems as the latter carry relatively lower maintenance costs. AI-based services, such as recommendation engines, are being added over these Cloud-based software systems so that clients can take their device interoperable applications closer to their end-users. In the context of BPM, small businesses are now realizing the advantages of offshoring their non-core business processes to these service providers. In particular, AI-based process transformation projects, such as robotic process automation, are being taken up in this space[11].

With a significant number of digital transformation use-cases arising across industrial sectors like logistics, banking and finance, health care, and retail, IT services organizations in the country are leveraging their client connections within these sectors to ramp up their emerging technology capabilities. These sectors have reached a substantive level of maturity in terms of their data gathering and management infrastructure and are considered ripe for building AI-based process improvement and customer-centric applications. Advanced Data Analytics, Natural Language Processing, Computer Vision, Robotic Process Automation, and Speech Recognition are some of the sub-domains of AI that are finding the greatest number of use-cases in such industries. According to a report on AI[12] published by the National Association of Software and Service Companies (NASSCOM, an industry association for the IT-BPM sector in India) in 2018, large IT services companies are steadily building in-house expertise in AI and are offering customizable AI solutions to its clients. IT giants, like TCS, Wipro, Infosys, HCL, and several others, have established AI research labs for this purpose over the past five to ten years. Demand for emerging technology solutions is also expected from small, medium, and large enterprises within the country. In India, spending on cloud solutions is estimated to grow at around 30% per annum with substantial demand coming in the form of a growing need for custom-made cloud solutions by the Indian enterprises[13]. Large IT service providers are also collaborating with start-ups to gradually develop Blockchain-based enterprise solutions for firms and supply chains within the country, mainly in sectors like banking and finance, public sector, telecommunication, health care, retail, and electric utilities. For this, they are working with regulators and public sector agencies in coming up with industry-wide technical standards concerning the development of such solutions[14]. With a conscious policy push for secondary sector growth in the country, enterprises in the manufacturing, automotive, transportation, and logistics sectors are looking for digital transformation solutions to get industry 4.0 ready and sustain themselves in the digital future[15]. Among these industries, manufacturing and auto-industry in particular, are expected to lead in the adoption of customized IoT solutions; as such solutions are foundational to the realization of industry 4.0 objectives[16].

1.1.2 Engineers and the Indian IT services industry

Engineering education is considered to be a stepping stone for entry into the IT services industry. As a result, the growth of this industry has resulted in a mushrooming of private, non-autonomous engineering colleges in the country. These colleges now account for around 90% of the total number of engineers graduating each year[17]. Although IT-related disciplines, like computer science engineering, are significantly aligned with the work requirements of this industry, engineering graduates from other engineering disciplines, like mechanical, electrical, and civil engineering, were also in demand. Engineering education in general was considered to impart a 'set of problem-solving skills, methods of thinking logically, and learning tools that help quick adaptation to changes in technology, domains, and tasks'[18]. Disciplinary backgrounds were less important compared to an individual's ability to adapt to changing tools and techniques adopted in the software industry, and as a result, the Indian engineers came to be known for their generic programming skillsets more than anything else[19]. As the IT industry now transitions into emerging technologies, the demand for skills beyond generic programming is increasing. New roles like data scientists are expected to have skills around data analytics, and expertise in grasping client's business use-cases, in addition to software programming[20]. IT services organizations are now recruiting new roles such as that of the data scientists, cloud architects, data engineers, cloud engineers in addition to their traditional software project management roles such as that of the business analysts and project managers, software engineers, and architects[21]. Recruitment for these new roles has significantly increased in the past decade and more so during the recent pandemic[22]. Reskilling the existing workforce toward these new technologies is also becoming unavoidable for IT services organizations at large[23].

Jobs like that of the data scientists are becoming the new aspirational jobs in this sector. Given the requirement of mathematical skills and client-relevant domain expertise in these new roles, engineers with background in non-IT disciplines, such as industrial engineering, mechanical and electrical engineering, who come with a substantive coursework in mathematics/statistics and their own domain-related subjects, are now seeing a renewed demand. Engineers were hitherto recruited by this industry in large numbers because it was felt that an engineering education helped them to quickly adapt and learn changing software programming technologies and tools. But the demand for skills from emerging technology projects looks characteristically different. Digital transformation solutions under the new industry 4.0 expectations are demanding interdisciplinary skillsets from engineers. For example, the entry of AI and IoT is calling for the expertise of mechanical and civil engineers in these technologies. Entrepreneurial mindsets, which can help to synergize these new technologies and develop industry-specific transformation solutions, are considered valuable. Especially in a country like India, non-IT engineers having these interdisciplinary skillsets could spearhead indigenous sectoral innovations[24]. In general, those having a combination of domain-specific skillsets along with programming and data-related skills are considered more suitable for building firm and industry-specific industry 4.0 solutions[25].

Although the demand for such interdisciplinary skills is expected to come up across all the industries, it is, at present, heavily concentrated within the Indian IT industry[26] – particularly for meeting the immediate short-term needs of their clients' businesses. To differentiate themselves in the short run, these clients want to grab the low-hanging emerging technology solutions such as offering predictive maintenance for the products they deliver to end-customers, incorporating recommendation systems for offering customized support services, etc. In the long run, they expect to integrate emerging technologies to streamline activities around their core businesses[27] – logistics, operations, sales, and service – to become more efficient, resilient, sustainable, and, more importantly, customer-centric. At present the clients are falling back on their long-standing service providers, the Indian IT services industry, for solving emerging technology use-cases at a relatively lower end in the value chain[28]. There is, however, ample scope for these service providers to scale up the value chain and support clients with the more complex use-cases around improvements of the latter's operational flexibility and business sustainability. This could certainly create a demand for the skills of non-IT engineers even within the IT services industry. They would be needed not just for their capability to adapt to software technologies, but also for their specialized domain expertise relevant to clients and their corresponding industry-specific digital transformation use-cases. For example, it is inefficient to rely on IT engineers alone to device information systems to monitor and control a complex production process in a manufacturing firm. Manufacturing/industrial or mechanical engineers might be better placed to elicit emerging technology use-cases in a bottom-up manner by considering the peculiarities around technical specifications and service expectations from the production process. The scenario we foresee is that the Indian IT industry will continue recruiting engineers of all types in large numbers, but seeing them less as just generic software programmers, and more as domain experts intending to utilize their domain knowledge in customized emerging technology projects. Currently, how far are our IT organizations geared to realize this scenario thus became the key question of our research.

1.2 Research objectives and key findings

The transition from delivering standardized software and business process services to customized emerging technology solutions poses new challenges for the Indian IT services organizations. Developing emerging technology solutions requires a different set of activities that may warrant an overhaul of the existing process workflows which these organizations have historically mastered[29]. Another challenge could stem from the interdisciplinary expectations that the emerging technology solutions require. For the IT services organizations, this would also imply providing sufficient opportunities to their workforce in terms of their career progression toward the emerging technology space so as to avoid issues like attrition, currently impacting this industry[30]. The objective of our study is to highlight and analyze the challenges facing the Indian IT services organizations around these two aspects. To achieve these objectives, we rely on an ethnographic study in one such organization and extend and connect our findings from this one organization to a broader set of similar IT services organizations operating in this industry. The meta-theoretical framework that guided us during our ethnography and helped extend our findings from this organization to the wider the Indian IT sector was that of Critical Realism (CR), which we elaborate in the Theoretical Appendix.

Our study shows that, despite the efforts to garner expertise around emerging technologies, the Indian IT services organizations face difficulty in moving up the client's value chain or even moving up the emerging technology value chain. Historically embedded workflows, designed to suit software service delivery, end up casting an inordinate and overarching influence on their emerging technology projects. This sway of workflows suited more to their extant software-related projects makes it difficult for the IT services organizations to renegotiate with their clients on workflows compatible with emerging technologies. We find that this poses a constraint for the movement of the Indian IT services organizations higher up the client's value chain – in terms of tackling digital transformation use-cases around their core production and operational activities. A majority of projects are related to further automating the outsourced IT-BPM services – around clients' non-core business activities such as IT support and maintenance, managing human resources, and customer relations – with emerging technologies, only to show a greater cost arbitrage for their clients. Another repercussion of this influence of software engineering principles on the emerging technology project workflows is also the difficulty these organizations face in moving up the emerging technology value chain. For example, Big-Tech companies, like IBM, Microsoft, Google, etc., are not only conducting cutting-edge research in emerging technologies but also building foundational platforms and generic products in this space. The Indian IT services organizations transitioning to emerging technologies, however, are largely dependent on these foundational platforms to build tailor-made emerging technology services to clients that are not easy to market as generic products. The path-dependency associated with the historically negotiated client-vendor relationship is constraining the Indian IT organizations from conducting cutting-edge research in the emerging technology space. Concerns related to explainability of emerging technology solutions and issues around billability of their development are further limiting their scope. Currently, the Indian IT organizations thus seem to be a long way off from developing industry-specific emerging technology solutions or making substantive innovations in the emerging technology space.

An advantage that the Indian IT services organizations have in their transition to emerging technology space, that often goes unnoticed, is the sheer volume and variety of skilled workforce, particularly that of their engineers. The diversity of skillsets that these engineers bring to the table, prima facie offers a great advantage to these organizations in scaling up the emerging technology value chain, on par with the Big-Tech companies like Google, IBM, Microsoft, and others. However, this calls for an organizational environment that facilitates a meaningful transposition of these skillsets while carrying out emerging technology innovations within these IT services organizations. We reiterate that for us, organizational environment has a very tangible technological and material implication – the work structures and workflows of these organizations that get executed in their various projects.

In the context of the challenge facing the Indian IT organizations, our study indicated a palpable mobility constraint for engineers from non-IT disciplines aspiring toward emerging technology roles, in particular, in the space of AI. While the organizational environment of IT services organizations was conducive to transform engineers from diverse disciplinary backgrounds into generic software engineers, this very environment acted as a constraint for non-IT engineers, wishing to transpose their domain expertise in emerging technology work. Many of these engineers were recruited for their expertise around data analytics and domain-specific skills learned during their engineering coursework. For example, industrial engineers were recruited for their data analytic skills to execute machine learning development. Their knowledge of production and business operations made them better suited to understanding the client's business use-cases. However, the dominance of software engineering principles on the emerging technology workflows overwhelmed these engineers working in beginner roles. These workflows meant that they were relegated largely with software programming tasks. It completely distanced them from a substantive engagement with the client's business domain and use-cases, where they could have contributed meaningfully. Their mobility aspirations toward taking on senior roles in the emerging technology space took a backseat. Drawing from our pre-study – an ethnography in a private engineering college near Bengaluru – we also highlight how this IT and non-IT divide has its roots in the Indian engineering education landscape, where engineers irrespective of their specializations are trained chiefly to land up with jobs in the mammoth IT services industry.

Fundamentally, therefore, our book argues that in any organization, the technology or the materiality underpinning workflows needs to be unpacked to understand the nature of work and issues of mobility around it. If organizations are beholden to specific workflows while designing and executing their projects, how does this hinder or ease the work done by their workforce? How does this change the nature of work? How does it impact the design and execution of newly evolving projects? The question about how workflows determine organizational environment and produce different outcomes sits at the center of our book. With the increasing demand for solutions around emerging technologies from India's IT services organizations, our study points to the need for these organizations to renegotiate workflows compatible with emerging technology projects. This will also prove to be conducive in meeting the mobility challenges of the non-IT engineers working on such projects and help IT services organizations in scaling up the value chain in the emerging technology space.

Based on our findings, we also draw implications for the Indian industrial and educational policies. For instance, the secondary sector in the country is dominated by informal enterprises and small and medium enterprises (SMEs) that lack sufficient capabilities toward digital transformation. Drawing from our study, we see two conundrums that need to be tackled by suitable policy interventions. Firstly, helping channelize the large number of skilled non-IT engineers in the IT services organizations whose domain expertise could be vital to the digital transformation of these SMEs in other industries. Here, our study hints that a meaningful integration of non-IT engineers in the Indian IT services organizations could propel the Indian IT services organizations in spearheading the digital transformation of other Indian industries. For policymakers, therefore, designing appropriate incentives for IT services organizations to look toward indigenous industrial sectors is an important aspect to note. The second conundrum is to build skilled workforce who can tackle digital transformation in different industry verticals, when most of the engineering colleges are largely catering to the employment demand from the IT industry and not so much elsewhere[31]. Engineers with interdisciplinary skillsets at the intersection of IT, emerging technologies, and industry-specific domain expertise are vital to the digital transformation of specific industries. In this regard, the educational policies need to make a note of the growing trend in engineering colleges toward employment predominantly in the IT sector and a consequent decline in the intake in non-IT engineering disciplines[32]. Education policies to incorporate IT and emerging technology courses significantly in the curriculum of non-IT engineering disciplines is one way to bring back their importance and contribute to a balanced contribution of engineers to different industrial sectors.

1.3 Overview of chapters

In Chapter 2, we introduce our ethnographic context, i.e., the AI research lab of this organization, in greater detail. We contextualize the significance of ITSO and its research lab to the transition of the Indian IT services industry toward emerging technologies and spell out the challenges pertaining to this industry which our ethnography seeks to decipher. We also discuss the details about work and workforce in this research lab, and the role played by a two-member research team – the ethnographer and mentor – in the context of this work ethnography.

In Chapter 3, we explore the challenges faced by IT services organizations as they transition toward delivering emerging technology solutions for the digital transformation needs of their clients. To this end, we first provide an overview of the nature of digital transformation experienced by client firms and the importance of their business context in achieving such a transformation. We discuss some key emerging technologies underpinning this digital transformation, in terms of value addition to one or more activities, and the manner in which these solutions could be envisaged. We then take the IT service provider's perspective and draw comparisons between software development and development of emerging technology solutions, in particular AI. Here we highlight the difference between their workflows to better contextualize our subsequent discussion about the execution of an AI project in an IT services organization. Drawing on our study of this organization, we highlight the key challenges that IT services organizations in India face as they transition into emerging technology space owing to their extant workflows. We point out as to how this impacts both, moving up in the client's value chain and moving up the AI value chain for the IT organization.

In Chapter 4, we look at the work in AI projects undertaken by ITSO's AI research lab through the perspective of its workforce, primarily the engineers. Paying attention to individuals occupying beginner roles in the space of AI and Cloud, we highlight their mobility constraints in accessing the aspirational roles around emerging technologies. Comparing the mobility prospects along educational and occupational backgrounds we discuss the conspicuous divide between those engineers having substantive expertise in software programming-related skills vis-à-vis those having only a limited exposure to them. The latter, despite their training in AI-related and domain-specific skills, are at a disadvantage accessing aspirational roles in the space of AI, vis-à-vis the former. The same, however, is not true in the case of beginner roles working in the space of software/cloud. Through our ethnographic findings in ITSO's AI research lab, we explain some of the generative mechanisms that gave rise to these differences. We connect this IT and non-IT divide in the Indian IT industry context with the Indian engineering education landscape by drawing from another ethnographic study that we conducted in an engineering college. Based on our findings, we briefly discuss the role that the Indian IT industry could play in bridging this divide.

In Chapter 5, we first provide a summary of our findings discussed in the previous chapters. A key insight among our findings was the need for the Indian IT services organizations to negotiate compatible workflows with their clients. Given that such a negotiation will inevitably happen within the newly unfolding client-vendor relationships in the era of emerging technologies, we provide some pointers in this regard, based on our ethnographic study. We then discuss the implications of our ethnographic findings to the Indian industrial and educational policy. Lastly, we conclude our study and highlight its limitations to motivate future work.

We observe that India is spearheading foundational digital innovations thanks to its enormous IT workforce. But the same is not translating into meaningful digital transformation of its remaining industrial sectors. Sectors, like manufacturing, energy, agriculture, etc., are awaiting meaningful emerging technology innovations conducive to their respective contexts. We see that the presence of a huge volume of non-IT engineering workforce within the Indian IT services organizations is a potential waiting to be tapped for the meaningful digital transition of non-IT sectors in the country. However, this calls for an imminent need to transform work processes within such organizations that allow the non–IT engineers to transpose their specialized skillsets. The Indian IT sector can thus play a leading role in the balanced digital-transformation-led growth of even other industrial sectors of the country. From an educational policy point of view, our study also indicates that, for these imaginations to come to fruition, a substantive incorporation of IT and emerging technologies into the curriculum of non-IT engineering disciplines is the need of the hour.

At the end, we provide a Theoretical Appendix for those readers interested in the theoretical underpinnings of our work ethnography. In this Theoretical Appendix, we introduce CR, the key meta-theoretical framework that was the peg around which our work ethnography was designed. We discuss its principles and its relevance as a philosophical basis for our research in an IT services organization. We also discuss how work ethnographies as a research methodology can be guided by the tenets of CR, and also providing a strong empirical basis for the latter. Subsequently, we articulate our findings through this framework and further highlight the significance of this framework in providing us a structure to draw insights from our ethnography. We end the appendix by providing some reflections on our ethnographic study.

Notes

1 MEITY. (2017). Fact sheet of IT & BPM industry. Ministry of Electronics and Information Technology, Government of India. https://www.meity.gov.in/content/fact-sheet-it-bpm-industry
2 Naidu, B. V. (2006). India: Emerging knowledge base of the 21st century. STPI: Delhi, 72; Jalote, P., & Natarajan, P. (2019). The growth and evolution of India's software industry. Communications of the ACM, 62(11), 64–69.
3 MEITY. (2017). Fact Sheet of IT & BPM Industry. Ministry of Electronics and Information Technology, Government of India. https://www.meity.gov.in/content/fact-sheet-it-bpm-industry
4 Arora, A., Arunachalam, V. S., Asundi, J., & Fernandes, R. (2001). The Indian software services industry. Research Policy, 30(8), 1267–1287.
5 Upadhya, C., & Vasavi, A. R. (2012). In an outpost of the global economy: Work and workers in India's information technology industry. Routledge.
6 Athreye, S. S. (2005). The Indian software industry and its evolving service capability. Industrial and Corporate Change, 14(3), 393–418; Dossani, R., & Kenney, M. (2007). The next wave of globalization: Relocating service provision to India. World Development, 35(5), 772–791.
7 Dopico, M., Gómez, A., De la Fuente, D., García, N., Rosillo, R., & Puche, J. (2016). A vision of industry 4.0 from an artificial intelligence point of view. Proceedings on the International Conference on Artificial Intelligence (ICAI), 407.
8 Fersht, P., & Snowdon, J. (2016). Making the leap from strategic to effective BPM. National Association of Software and Service Companies. https://www.nasscom.in/knowledge-center/publications/making-leap-effective-strategic-bpm
9 NASSCOM. (2018). Artificial intelligence primer. National Association of Software and Service Companies.
10 NASSCOM. (2017). IT-BPM strategic review. National Association of Software and Service Companies.

11 Fersht, P., & Snowdon, J. (2016). Making the leap from strategic to effective BPM. National Association of Software and Service Companies. https://www.nasscom.in/knowledge-center/publications/making-leap-effective-strategic-bpm

12 NASSCOM. (2018). Artificial intelligence primer. National Association of Software and Service Companies.

13 NASSCOM. (2018). Talent Demand and Supply Report, AI and Big Data Analytics. National Association of Software and Service Companies.

14 NASSCOM. (2019). NASSCOM Avasant India Blockchain Report 2019.

15 NASSCOM. (2019). Industry 4.0: A primer on startup driven industrial stories.

16 NASSCOM. (2017). Report by Deloitte and NASSCOM on, the Internet of Things: Revolution in the making.

17 Banerjee, R., & Muley, V. P. (2007). Engineering education in India. Report to Energy Systems Engineering, IIT Bombay, Sponsored by Observer Research Foundation, September, 14; Thakur, A., & Mantha, S. (2021). Modi Govt's HEC can't just be UGC with new label. Engineering still needs its own regulator.

18 Arora, A., Arunachalam, V. S., Asundi, J., & Fernandes, R. (2001). The Indian software services industry. Research Policy, 30(8), 1267–1287.

19 Upadhya, C., & Vasavi, A. R. (2012). In an outpost of the global economy: Work and workers in India's information technology industry. Routledge.

20 Davenport, T. H., & Patil, D. J. (2012). Data scientist. Harvard Business Review, 90(5), 70–76.

21 NASSCOM. (2019). Uncovering the true value of AI, executive AI playbook for enterprises. National Association of Software and Service Companies.

22 Baruah, A. (2020). IT sector hiring in new-age skills to pick up in 2021. https://www.livemint.com. https://www.livemint.com/companies/news/it-sector-hiring-in-new-age-skills-to-pick-up-in-2021-11605686860932.html

23 NASSCOM. (2018). Talent Demand and Supply Report, AI and Big Data Analytics. National Association of Software and Service Companies.

24 Indian Express. (2022, July 4). Anil Sahasrabudhe at Idea Exchange: 'The economy can't run only on computer science or electronics, it requires civil and mechanical engineering, too.' Retrieved July 13, 2022, from The Indian Express website: https://indianexpress.com/article/idea-exchange/anil-sahasrabudhe-idea-exchange-the-economy-session-8007078/

25 Roy, M., & Roy, A. (2021). The rise of interdisciplinarity in engineering education in the era of industry 4.0: Implications for management practice. IEEE Engineering Management Review, 49(3), 56–70.

26 NASSCOM. (2018). Talent Demand and Supply Report, AI and Big Data Analytics. National Association of Software and Service Companies.

27 Porter (1985). See Michael Porter's conceptualization of value chain and activities within it (primary activities include inbound logistics, operations, outbound logistics, marketing and sales, service). The competitive advantage: Creating and sustaining superior performance.

28 References: NASSCOM. (2018). Talent Demand and Supply Report, AI and Big Data Analytics. National Association of Software and Service Companies; Fersht, P., & Snowdon, J. (2016). Making the leap from strategic to effective BPM. National Association of Software and Service Companies. https://www.nasscom.in/knowledge-center/publications/making-leap-effective-strategic-bpm.

29 Amershi, S., Begel, A., Bird, C., DeLine, R., Gall, H., Kamar, E., … Zimmermann, T. (2019). Software engineering for machine learning: A case study. 2019 IEEE/ACM 41st International Conference on Software Engineering: Software Engineering in Practice (ICSE-SEIP), 291–300. IEEE.

30 Singh, A. (2022). Indian IT industry battling all-time high attrition rate. The Week. https://www.theweek.in/news/biz-tech/2022/05/19/indian-it-industry-battling-all-time-high-attrition-rate.html

31 Kamath, R., Venumuddala, V., & Manjunath, A. (2022). National Education Policy needs to strengthen core engineering disciplines for the success of industry 4.0. https://www.forbesindia.com/article/iim-bangalore/national-education-policy-needs-to-strengthen-core-engineering-disciplines-for-the-success-of-industry-40/74023/1

32 AICTE. (2018). Engineering education in India: Short and medium term perspectives. All India Council for Technical Education, Government of India.

2   Research context

2.1 Research context – AI research lab in an IT services organization (ITSO)

IT services organizations operating from India have been dealing traditionally with delivery of custom software and business process management (BPM) services, outsourced by their global clients. Concurrently, the past decade has seen digital transformation strategies becoming vital for businesses to sustain their competitive advantage. But not all firms have the wherewithal to invest into these technologies. This is making many of them take a relook at the Indian IT services organizations for outsourcing solutions related to digitization. The IT organization, where we carried out our work ethnography, was one such organization facing this renewed demand for services around emerging technologies from its clients. One of us, whom we shall call the ethnographer, formally joined as an intern in the emerging technology research lab of this IT services organization, which we shall refer to as ITSO. The other researcher in this research team mentored the ethnographer from outside of ITSO and the study is therefore a collaborative effort of this two-member research team.

ITSO is situated in Bengaluru, India, a city that is called the 'Silicon Valley' of India both for its established IT and IT enabled services (ITeS) organizations and also for its growing technology entrepreneurs[1]. ITSO was set up in the late 1990s and is well-known for providing outsourcing services to global clients in the areas of custom software development and/or maintenance, BPM, and IT infrastructure management. It also provides strategy development and consulting services in all of these areas. ITSO offers services to clients across many industry verticals. Among these, banking and finance, health care, government, manufacturing, transportation, FMCG, and retail are predominant. It ranks within the top 200 of the Fortune-India 500 companies[2] and operates from all the major metropolitan cities in India and has global presence in over 15 other countries in North America, Australia, and Europe. As of FY 2019-20 it boasts a workforce of close to 30,000 employees, and its revenues exceed a billion US dollars.

DOI: 10.1201/9781003324355-2

2.1.1 ITSO's AI research lab

Around the year 2014, ITSO established a research lab to garner expertise in emerging technologies, mainly to address the digital transformation needs of their long-standing clients. At present it works on technologies, such as Artificial Intelligence (AI), Cloud, Blockchain, Internet of Things (IoT), and Quantum Computing, which we elaborate on in Chapter 3. With the help of this lab, ITSO is now providing emerging-technology-enhanced IT-BPM services to its clients, largely in the space of AI and Cloud. We therefore call this lab as the AI research lab.

AI- and Cloud-enhanced IT-BPM services are the mainstay for this research lab. In the context of cloud, ITSO relies on its historically grown expertise in handling clients' applications hosted in legacy systems to provide modernization services around adjusting such applications for Cloud. Clients find it attractive; as such services eliminate the need for managing legacy systems and reduce significantly the cost of managing or maintaining IT infrastructure and resources. While Cloud offerings are undertaken by many other software units within ITSO, what makes the contribution of AI research lab stand out is the provision of AI-enhanced and Cloud-compatible custom software solutions to clients. The lab promises a capability to incorporate AI into existing software solutions so that clients can better incorporate the preferences of their respective customers while offering their products/services. ITSO also has many independent offshore development centers, each catering to the BPM services of a specific client. These offshore development centers are manned by business process outsourcing (BPO) workforce consisting of domain experts, software architects, software engineers, and a huge number of data-entry and call-center operators. The latter helps ITSO undertake customer interaction services and other services driven by labor and cost arbitrage. In the past decade, the BPO workforce at ITSO are also being trained to handle advanced business process services around the customization and maintenance of third-party enterprise platforms or other proprietary platforms hosted by the clients. The AI research lab specializes in augmenting these new business process services with AI and Cloud so that clients can achieve efficiency, scalability, and flexibility in their business operations.

ITSO projects that its emerging-technology-augmented software and business process services help clients to adjust rapidly to the changing market circumstances and get future-ready. In addition to the usual IT-BPM services, ITSO also manages clients' IT infrastructure (like data centers). Here, the AI- and Cloud-based enhancements are expected to add to the IT infrastructure's efficiency, agility, and security. Utilizing its domain experts, software engineers, and skilled emerging technology workforce of the AI research lab, ITSO also promises to offer strategy consulting services to clients around emerging-technology-driven digital transformation. In the context of Blockchain, it promises consulting services for clients to design, develop, and run enterprise Blockchain applications – at present limited to industry verticals such as finance, health care, and logistics. In the context of IoT, it promises industry-specific IoT strategy consulting services covering conception, prototype creation, development, testing, and wherever relevant the strategy to combine other emerging technologies like AI, Cloud, and Blockchain. Here it projects specialization in industry verticals such as health care and logistics. The AI research lab is also experimenting with Quantum Computing mainly to get a hands-on expertise of working with existing open-source Quantum Computing platforms such as IBM's Qiskit[3].

2.1.2 Work and workforce in the AI research lab

As mentioned before, a majority of projects undertaken by the research lab were related to AI, and, in this regard, there were two kinds of projects. The first kinds of projects are related to research around AI. These projects are entirely ideated and developed by the data scientists of the lab. They work on training advanced machine learning (ML) models on off-the-shelf data available either as open-source benchmark datasets or non-confidential data from previous projects. In addition to AI, these data scientists are also building research expertise for their lab around other technologies such as Blockchain, IoT, and Quantum Computing. Such expertise becomes vital for ITSO's emerging-technology-based consulting services in general, and most importantly in attracting clients toward their AI solutions. The work done in this research only projects end up as Intellectual Property (IPs) for this lab, meant to be customized or reused for future projects.

The second kinds of projects which are the majority, are related to automating portions of manual, data-entry work performed by the BPO workforce in the offshore development centers of ITSO or of a client's other service providers. These projects are the mainstay for this lab and also an important source for building proprietary IPs around AI. For clients, such projects addressed an increased need for digitalization within their customer-centric activities, since it reduced reliance on manual data-entry workforce. By capturing employee tacit knowledge, it helped mitigate knowledge transfer challenges during attrition. A majority of these projects are related to the application of AI to automate the digitalization of a client's process logs or contractual documents by extracting critical information and storing it online. These projects require processing unstructured textual data and making it conducive for training ML algorithms. They fall within the subdomain of ML called Natural Language Processing (NLP). Expertise within other subdomains of ML, such as Computer Vision, Speech Processing, Graph Machine Learning, etc., is currently research-driven – but the team lead believes that client-centric projects in these subdomains are not far away. Managing software development in Cloud was already a strength of ITSO, as its software units have already been handling projects to migrate many of the legacy software applications from client's on-premise servers to the Cloud. This expertise also comes handy for the AI research lab to deploy their solution stack, mainly their AI-related IPs, onto Cloud. Such deployment allows the lab to offer turnkey services around AI, not just for the intended clients, but also for the general users many of whom could be their prospective clients. Amazon Web Services (AWS), Google Cloud Platform (GCP), and Azure were the three major cloud platforms where ITSO and its lab deployed their solution stack.

This lab was established as a separate unit by gathering members from its traditional software units and recruiting employees with skills in emerging technologies. It consisted of close to 30 members covering technical and managerial roles. Apart from the team lead, there were other managerial roles such as the business analysts and project managers. Technical roles encompassed data engineers, data scientists, software engineers, cloud engineers, and cloud architects. Cloud and software experts from adjacent software teams were also involved in the AI projects whenever required. In client-focused AI projects of the research lab, managerial roles, mainly the business analysts, conduct client-facing activities and at the same time oversee the work of their subordinates like the data engineers who execute the project. Project managers are responsible for allocating technical resources (like allocation of costly cloud storage and third-party applications) and human resources for a particular project. Data scientists undertake research activities and also informally guide data engineers in the context of the latter's AI/ML work on a client project. Cloud and software engineers are guided by respective architects and are responsible for integrating AI components, building front-end interfaces, and deploying the resulting solutions over Cloud for clients to access. In the context of AI augmentation of BPO work, the BPO teams are responsible for manual validation of the AI solution outputs. Figure 2.1

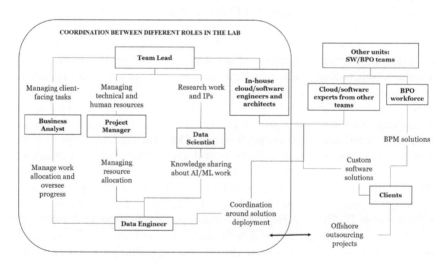

Figure 2.1 AI Research Lab, ITSO: Key work roles and the coordination

summarizes the purpose of coordination between different roles in the context of ITSO's AI research lab.

The AI research lab stands out among other teams or units at ITSO because many new joinees of ITSO aspire to work here. The new joinees, mostly engineers from diverse backgrounds, undergo rigorous three-month training and evaluation and are allocated to different teams based on their evaluation scores. Even some of the senior roles from other teams consider the work at AI research lab to be cutting-edge and are therefore keen to make a transition to this lab. This lab also has many special provisions and facilities compared to other teams at ITSO. In the Bengaluru office, ITSO had two dedicated floors in a seven-storied building from where it operated. One floor is completely dedicated and tightly secured for its offshore development center from where the BPO workforce handled BPM services for one of ITSO's clients from logistics vertical. BPO workforce were not allowed to carry even a pen or a pencil into their workplace, and their attendance is tightly monitored. They are shut off completely from the outside world as their mobile phones are to be left at the entrance of the BPO office. On the other floor, one side is allocated to teams around software development, IT administration and support, and human resources. They are again tightly regulated for their attendance and in terms of their access to the outside world. Although they are allowed to carry mobile phones, they did not have open Internet access or a flexibility to work from home (WFH). A transition to WFH mandated by the pandemic was operationally difficult for these teams. Compared to these other teams hosted on this floor, the AI research lab had special provisions in terms of flexible work timings, open Internet access, dedicated whiteboards, and discussion rooms for research work and collaboration. All the members of the lab were seated together and their cubicles directly faced the team lead's cabin. In office, informal interactions and banter between the members of the lab were par for the course, compared to the remaining teams hosted on this floor.

2.1.3 Work ethnography in the AI research lab

Our work ethnography in the ITSO's AI research lab was designed to infer two possible challenges that the IT services organizations venturing into the space of emerging technologies might face. The first one is organization related – the challenges that organizations like ITSO face as they negotiate workflows to suit the new emerging technology projects in an offshore outsourcing context. The development and delivery of emerging technology solutions is still a new endeavor for these organizations, and the maturity of their associated workflows is still a work-in-progress in the industry in general[4]. The second one is related to workforce in the research lab – the challenges concerning mobility of engineers in these organizations toward their aspirational emerging technology roles in this industry. Many such roles are receiving a lot of hype[5] in the industry, and are attracting individuals with interdisciplinary skillsets[6], not only around these technologies, but also with software engineering skills, and industry-specific business domain knowledge.

The ethnographer formally joined ITSO as an intern, to work in the AI research lab for the period between January and May 2020[7]. He/she had to go through all the relevant joining formalities that IT services organization would require. Getting work and educational backgrounds verified, obtaining an identity card and getting the cubicle allocated, going through internal trainings to navigate the company's human resources portal, etc., were some of them. There were other training modules about an employee's appropriate behavior at work, dos and don'ts during interaction with clients, training on norms about complying with general data protection regulation (GDPR), etc., which the ethnographer had to do parallelly with work, after joining. The ethnographer was introduced by the team lead to other members of the lab as an intern and a researcher who would draw policy-focused insights relevant to the IT industry and mobility of its workforce from his/her internship experience. The ethnographer's role in the team was decided by the team lead based on educational and occupational backgrounds. Mainly, the exposure to ML in doctoral coursework made the team lead to assign the ethnographer two key responsibilities: (1) to work full-time during the internship period on a running AI project, and (2) talk to the team members about current and the previous AI projects, and present the team with an emergent workflow along with its constituent activities that this lab has negotiated with their clients. Our research team – the ethnographer and mentor – also gave regular presentations to the members of this lab about the findings from our ethnography, and these presentations helped us triangulating our research findings based on the opinions expressed by different members.

A typical day in office for the ethnographer started with breakfast with some of the colleagues from the lab in the office canteen. After breakfast, the ethnographer went on to performing the day-to-day project-related work. It was usual to meet up occasionally between work and coffee breaks, and have casual conversations around cubicles. The more formal conversations were for whitepaper discussions and the weekly project status meetings. In the afternoon, the ethnographer went to lunch with some of the team members. Frequently, they took an after-lunch walk around the ITSO's building and came back again to work till evening. Owing to the pandemic-imposed nationwide lockdown that happened close to the end of March, ITSO enforced WFH for most of its teams; as a result, the ethnographer worked for about three months in the office and slightly over a month from home. Other than the formal project status meetings and preset meetings with other team members, WFH also implied that all the informal interactions that the ethnographer had with other team members were no more part of the ethnographer's typical working day.

The ethnographer interacted with almost all the members of this lab who occupied various technical and managerial roles across software engineering and emerging technologies. Informal discussions around employee cubicles, interactions during project status meetings, breakfast, coffee, and lunch breaks, birthday parties and farewell functions, etc., helped the ethnographer bond as a member of this team, as against being seen as an outsider. Thanks to the work in a running AI project as an intern, the ethnographer worked closely with the following members: Kamal the business analyst-cum-project manager, Sruthi and Krishna who were the data scientists in this lab, Yuvraj the cloud architect, Harish and Vinod the data engineers, and Sameer and Javed the cloud/software engineers. Whenever possible, the ethnographer used to take down short memory markers on observations concerning rationale for the projects, work roles, their interactions, a background of employees, their current work roles, and future aspirations. Depending on the convenience, such short memory markers were then entered into a note-taking application on the cell phone or a physical notebook. Elaborating on such short memory markers each day after work enabled the ethnographer to build a corpus of daily field notes that was shared every week with the mentor.

The mentor's role in this ethnography was crucial. Given the ethnographer's engagement with the project, the ethnographer frequently got engrossed in the day-to-day project work and its associated deadlines. This posed a risk to our study where we could lose the necessary perspective to extend the findings beyond this lab or take a more distanced view of the complexities of its work. The mentor took an etic perspective and nudged the ethnographer to refocus attention every week toward our study's broader goals, thereby helping the ethnographer to consciously dis-embed him/herself from work, whenever possible, and connect the day-to-day observations (emic) with the ongoings beyond this organization. The former also critically perused through the field notes, prepared and communicated reflections based on it, and helped the ethnographer to better contextualize and connect the day-to-day field observations in relation to emerging technologies and the Indian IT industry in general. Weekly discussions between the mentor and the ethnographer clarified the directions in which we could make such connections. The resulting field notes that formed the basis of our study were therefore a synthesis of these emic and etic perspectives shaped by this two-member research team. The field notes captured the essence of (a) several unstructured interviews (UI) and impromptu conversations (IC) that the ethnographer carried out with the members of this lab, and (b) observations and internalized experiences of the ethnographer as he/she worked on a running AI project (project experience or PE) with other team members. Our ethnographic field notes spanning the four-month internship period ran into 114 single-spaced pages in Microsoft Word, which amounted to over 80,000 words. Table 2.1 summarizes the overview of our ethnographic data gathered in the form of field notes during our ethnography at ITSO's research lab. Although the ethnographer interacted with almost all the team members in this four-month period, there were some of them with whom the ethnographer interacted almost on a daily basis. In this table, we also provide additional information about such interactions.

Table 2.1 Overview of data-sources constituting Field Notes

Work roles	#	Experience range	Qualifications	Source of data	Remarks about specific individuals
Data Engineers (Beginner technical roles in the AI space)	12	Between 6 months – 3 years	Masters/B. Tech	PE, UI, IC	The ethnographer worked along with **Harish** and **Vinod**, two data engineers, on the ongoing AI project. The tasks assigned to the ethnographer were also similar to the ones assigned to these two engineers. Three of us had to present our work done during the weekly project status meetings. This allowed the ethnographer to interact with these two regularly. The ethnographer was part of several conversations with them about the intricacies of the current project, their work interests, and their hobbies. Of the two, Harish came with only a working knowledge in software programming, whereas Vinod was an expert at it.
Data Scientists (Senior technical roles in the AI space)	5	Between 4–7 years	PhD/ Masters	PE, UI, IC	Out of these data scientists, the ethnographer closely interacted with two – **Sruthi and Krishna. Sruthi is** a senior data scientist and Krishna, relatively junior. The team lead's assigned task around project workflows led the ethnographer to conduct unstructured interviews or discussions with these two. Discussions with Sruthi happened in multiple instances, and they were primarily around the intricacies around AI project work, challenges facing the lab in the context of AI projects, and the steps being taken to overcome them. With Krishna, the ethnographer conducted an unstructured interview about a previous AI project's workflow. Krishna also helped the ethnographer with programming-related bottlenecks that the latter faced during the day-to-day work. Some of the discussions with Sruthi and Krishna were also around the differences between traditional SW and AI projects.
Cloud/ software Engineers (Beginner technical roles)	5	Between 6 months – 3 years	B. Tech	UI, IC	The ethnographer got introduced to **Sameer** and **Javed,** the two cloud/software engineers through the two data engineers – Harish and Vinod. Conversations with these two helped the ethnographer decipher the intricacies around the deployment of AI components in the Cloud. In addition to Sameer and Javed, there were two more in-house cloud/software engineers with whom the ethnographer interacted regularly. The latter occupied cubicles adjacent to the ethnographer. This helped the ethnographer participate in several informal conversations that were happening around their cubicles. Most of these conversations were around the software engineering aspects related to integration and deployment.

(Continued)

Table 2.1 Overview of data-sources constituting Field Notes (*Continued*)

Work roles	#	Experience range	Qualifications	Source of data	Remarks about specific individuals
Business Analysts (Senior Managerial Roles)	2	Between 3–15 years	MBA/ Extensive industry experience	PE, UI, IC	Of the two, the ethnographer formally worked under **Kamal** who was a senior business analyst. In the current project he was also the project manager. The key topics of discussion with him were around our research insights and about the current project work. Kamal also oversaw the work done by the ethnographer, Harish and Vinod – the data engineers, during the weekly project status meetings. This allowed the ethnographer an opportunity to witness the conversations around the progress of the project that Kamal initiated. Kamal also regularly carried out visits to the offshore development centers of ITSO to understand how the BPO workforce were responding to a particular client's work. Accompanying him to breakfast and lunch regularly allowed the ethnographer to understand the significance of BPO work and workforce in the context of AI projects taken up by this lab.
Cloud/ software Architect (Senior Technical roles)	2	Between 7–15 years	MBA/ Extensive industry experience	UI, IC	The ethnographer accompanied **Yuvraj**, a cloud architect and Kamal, the project manager, to lunch on a daily basis. These lunch conversations between the two of them were invaluable for the ethnographer to make sense of the AI projects, client-vendor relationships, and other aspects related to work in this research lab.
Managers/ Assistant VPs, VP/ Team Lead (Senior Managerial Roles)	4	Between 2–10 years	PhD	PE, UI, IC	Apart from Kamal, **the team lead** also occasionally attended the project status meetings. While Kamal oversaw the specifics, the team lead was interested in high-level status of the project progress. The ethnographer along with the mentor also presented the insights gathered from our ethnography to the team lead and other members of the team. Their comments and queries helped in refining our understanding about the work undertaken in this lab.

Note: Out of the five cloud/software engineers shown here, two are from an adjacent team who frequently work on the projects undertaken by this lab. Unless explicitly stated, these two software engineers are treated as being part of the lab for the purpose of this study.

2.1.4 A precursor study – ethnography in an engineering college

As a precursor to the aforementioned work ethnography at ITSO's AI research lab, the ethnographer also conducted another ethnographic study in a private engineering college as a tutor in Data Analytics. This ethnography helped us to make connections between the IT industry and the dominant suppliers of its workforce – the engineering colleges. The particular objective guiding this ethnography was to understand the mobility pathways that the IT industry had created for prospective engineers from different disciplines within these colleges. Apart from the ethnographer and the mentor, Manjunath, another PhD student, was also part of this project[8]. To conduct this ethnography, we formally approached the head of the Electronics Engineering department of this private engineering college near Bengaluru and informed her about our research objectives and permission to conduct tutorial sessions on Data Analytics to students once every week. She forwarded our request to the principal of this college, who, after discussing the motives and objectives behind our ethnography, and the outline of our tutorial sessions, granted the formal permission to undertake these sessions. The sessions were arranged by the head of the electronics engineering department around 12–1 pm every Thursday for third-year electronics students for one-semester duration (between June and November 2019). Our ethnography in this college relied entirely on participant observations, IC, and UI with students, faculty, and other staff, outside these tutorial sessions every Thursday during the said period. Although our study is largely based on the primary ethnography as discussed above, the ethnography in this engineering college was an important precursor as it helped the ethnographer to grasp the nuances of effectively conducting an ethnography and also helped to better contextualize the connections between the IT industry and engineering colleges. We cover more details about this ethnography and its relevance to our primary ethnography in Chapter 4.

Notes

1 References: https://edition.cnn.com/2012/12/06/tech/bangalore-india-internet-access
2 https://www.fortuneindia.com/fortune-500?year=2021
3 https://qiskit.org/
4 Sculley, D., Holt, G., Golovin, D., Davydov, E., Phillips, T., Ebner, D., Chaudhary, V., Young, M., Crespo, J.-F., & Dennison, D. (2015). Hidden technical debt in machine learning systems. Advances in Neural Information Processing Systems, 2503–2511; Bilgeri, D., Gebauer, H., Fleisch, E., & Wortmann, F. (2019). Driving process innovation with IoT field data. MIS Quarterly Executive, 18, 191–207; Bumblauskas, D., Mann, A., Dugan, B., & Rittmer, J. (2020). A Blockchain use case in food distribution: Do you know where your food has been? International Journal of Information Management, 52, 102008.
5 For example: Data scientist. Reference: Davenport, T. H., & Patil, D. J. (2012). Data scientist. Harvard Business Review, 90(5), 70–76.
6 Roy, M., & Roy, A. (2021). The rise of interdisciplinarity in engineering education in the era of industry 4.0: Implications for management practice. IEEE Engineering Management Review, 49(3), 56–70.

7 We formally approached the head of the AI research lab at ITSO (on the 24th of September 2019) with a request for an internship and permission to conduct our ethnographic research. The head of this lab allowed the ethnographer to apply for a contract intern position in their team, and after the formal interview process and background checks, he/she was formally recruited. In order to avoid the problem of receiving additional financial assistance from the company beyond the ethnographer's research stipend, we applied for a separate research project code for this ethnography within our institute and provided the details of the project account to the company so as to redirect these additional funds. We also enquired if there was a possibility of not to avail any financial support from the company during this period. But, because they had to abide by the minimum pay mandates as a company, the company formally offered Rs. 20,000 in total for the four-month period as per their offer letter. For contract employees in their company, the payment is released only upon initiation from the employee end. Because of the said circumstances, the ethnographer preferred not to initiate this process during the internship. The ethnographer received a formal offer letter from the company to join in the second week of January 2020. Immediately after this approval from the company, we formally initiated the process of reviewing our ethnography through our Institutional Review Board (IRB) at IIMB. We passed additional information about our ethnography as required by the IRB to the head of the AI research lab and other members of this lab and sought their approval. After submitting these necessary approvals back to the IRB, our project was finally approved. The study ID for this ethnography project is "IIMB-IRB#15". Adhering to the IRB requirements, we maintained complete confidentiality about the company and its people in this study. After the completion of our study at the end of May 2020, we have provided the IRB with information about the completion of our ethnography.

8 Refer to: https://www.forbesindia.com/article/iim-bangalore/national-education-policy-needs-to-strengthen-core-engineering-disciplines-for-the-success-of-industry-40/74023/1

3 Emerging technology work in an Indian IT services organization

The global demand for emerging technology solutions is rising as firms across industry sectors are driven by the unceasing wave of digital transformation. For firms in sectors like manufacturing, to sustain in the times of this fourth industrial revolution or industry 4.0, it has become imperative to transform their hitherto rigid production systems to be more efficient and flexible. Efficient in terms of meeting the sustainability goals around energy and resource usage, and flexible in terms of meeting demand fluctuations[1]. To achieve such a transformation, firms require synergizing emerging technologies, like Artificial Intelligence (AI), Cloud, Internet of Things (IoT), Blockchain, and many others, to suit their specific business contexts. In particular, AI has become central to such a transformation with other technologies providing the necessary foundational infrastructure to realize AI-based smart applications. For example, in the context of industry 4.0, IoT provides the necessary communication, networking, and control mechanisms to gather data from sensors and other devices in the production process[2]. Such data will require data management infrastructure locally (often termed as edge), or remotely (in the Cloud). Blockchain can ensure the protection of sensitive data and enhance accountability and trust between transacting stakeholders within and beyond the firm. Built on the foundation set by some or all of these technologies, and depending on the current levels of process maturity in a firm, AI can help in realizing applications around process monitoring, optimization, and control in the context of industry 4.0[3]. This synergy of several of these emerging technologies, which we describe in Section 3.1, is gradually leading to the blurring of boundaries between cyber and physical systems.

This transition for the Indian IT industry from delivering standardized software and business process services to customized emerging technology solutions is not straightforward. Among many challenges, our study sheds light upon two of them. Differences in the emerging technology development workflows from their extant software workflows and the scarcity of skilled emerging technology workforce to fill the newly emerging work roles. Emerging technology solutions are characterized by activities that may not fit well into the currently mature software development workflows[4], which the

DOI: 10.1201/9781003324355-3

Indian IT services companies are known for. New work roles in the emerging technology domain are expected to possess interdisciplinary skillsets in terms of having technical expertise at handling emerging technologies and software development on the one hand, and substantive sectoral expertise on the other[5]. This is particularly crucial to the development of context-specific emerging technology solutions for different kinds of enterprises[6]. In this chapter, we focus on the first constraint mentioned above – the challenge posed by the nature of its extant workflows in carrying out emerging technology projects. The second constraint will be covered in the next chapter. Before going into the details pertaining to our observations from our work ethnography, we provide a broad overview of emerging technology solutions from the perspective of clients. Subsequently, we take the IT service provider's perspective to highlight some important differences between delivering software solutions and emerging technology solutions. With regard to the latter, we give greater attention to AI solution development because it is one of those emerging technologies around which several outsourcing projects are being taken up by firms in the Indian IT industry – including ITSO. Many of these findings will also apply to other emerging technology solutions, as they too are fraught with the same problems. A background about these is vital to understand the constraints related to workflows that IT services organizations in India will have to overcome for effectively transitioning into the emerging technology space.

3.1 Emerging technology solutions

Technologies historically have brought revolutionary changes to the way production has been carried out. Increase in mechanization and advent of steam engines led to the first industrial revolution. Intensive use of electricity and mass production techniques, mastered by companies like Ford and General Motors, paved the way for a second industrial revolution. Increased usage of Information Technologies and a consequent push for widespread digitalization characterized the third industrial revolution. The growing importance of emerging technologies, such as AI, IoT, Cloud, Blockchain, and others, is fueling a fourth industrial revolution or industry 4.0. Shifting from rigidly arranged production activities toward greater flexibility in adjusting to the changing customer needs, while keeping sustainability concerns around resource and energy efficiency in view, characterize this new revolution[7].

At its core, industry 4.0 pushes the limits of customer-centricity, which firms can aim to achieve. From mass production, firms are now expected to move toward mass customization – i.e., manufacturing individually customized products while maintaining economies of scale[8]. They are pushed toward catering to almost individualized customer demands by not just building customized products, but also offering a combination of product and support services to differentiate themselves and remain competitive in a constantly changing market scenario. With a combination of technologies, such as IoT, Cloud, Blockchain, AI, and others, industry 4.0 envisages smart products which control their own manufacturing process and smart factories which self-organize themselves for customized product configurations different for different customers. Smart products are capable of communicating information about their build status during production and usage status during consumption. IoT and Cloud technologies play a vital role in facilitating such capabilities. Self-organizing smart factories can perceive their environment and act in such a way as to increase their chances of success and AI is crucial in building this 'self-consciousness' into a firm's production systems. Blockchain can help with transparency and traceability of the products through different activities in a firm's value chain – activities such as inbound logistics, production and operations, outbound logistics, marketing and sales, and service[9]. This will help attract customers who place more trust in a product when its provenance and tracking information are transparently communicated.

3.1.1 Importance of a firm's business context in digital transformation

The current landscape of emerging technology solutions is dominated by use-cases around improving transactional activities that firms conduct with upstream suppliers or downstream customers. A vast number of digital transformation use-cases are centered around improvements to logistics, marketing and sales, and support. With the expectations of industry 4.0, and a need to remain sustainable and competitive in their markets, firms are also seeking emerging technology solutions to support their core production and operational activities.

At the onset it should be realized that not all the firms have the wherewithal to carry out advanced emerging technology solutions in-house. Large enterprises have deep pockets for diversification into new technologies unlike the Small and Medium Enterprises (SMEs) which often lack such access due to the ownership by a small set of individuals and less collateral[10]. SMEs work in a specific area of expertise and lack alliances with industry consortia or academic institutions. They have fewer but highly specialized products to manage, a selected segment of customers, and a specific set of suppliers/vendors to whom they outsource some of their activities. Their collaborative network is therefore small and is characterized by extreme dependence on few suppliers/vendors[11]. Although their employees are known for their wide expertise across a range of activities associated with their business, they often lack supervised training, and access to shared knowledge about other product value chains in their industry[12]. Compliance with standards is also quite low in SMEs as there is often a risk of disclosing production and operational activities which could differentiate them from their competitors[13]. Diversification decisions are also largely driven by their decision-makers, and as a result SMEs often lack the organizational culture and strategy required to experiment with emerging technologies compared to large corporations[14]. Because of these financial, knowledge, and organizational constraints, SMEs will rely most on outsourcing for the adoption of emerging technologies[15].

For the Indian IT organizations to whom these activities are outsourced, it is imperative that dealing with a variety of clients, they build solutions that can be customizable for their specific needs and contexts. Solutions have to take into account the maturity of their extant processes or activities and what level of technology adoption would be suitable for them. In the context of industry 4.0, Gokalp et al.[16] identify five aspect dimensions that need to be strengthened sequentially to make a firm industry 4.0 ready. These are asset management, data governance, application management, process transformation, and organizational alignment. A firm could start first with managing its assets by gathering requisite information about its location and status through the use of appropriate sensor, communication, networking, and storage technologies. Once this aspect is strengthened, a firm could then strengthen its data governance mechanisms by streamlining activities related to data gathering, and building data analytics pipelines to inform decision-making. Firms should then build information systems to manage the underlying data and associated devices that generate them. Such information systems need to have the flexibility to deploy applications to manage information flow and, if possible, also manage the value chain activities that the firm performs. Such infrastructure, when in place, will help a firm to achieve process transformation wherein the hitherto activities around input acquisition, production planning and flow, sale and distribution, etc., could be carried out predominantly in the digital space. These virtual or simulated process representations are often termed in substantive literature as the digital twin. In the last stage, a firm has to align its organizational structure, strategies, and human resource management, with these technological underpinnings so as to realize the true value of digital transformation. Emerging technologies will therefore have to be appropriately synergized depending on the firm's context, and its current process maturity stage.

Table 3.1 summarizes the above discussion.

3.1.2 Developing different emerging technology solutions

The foregoing discussion summarizes the nature of a holistic digital/process transformation that a typical firm might look up to. For IT service providers looking to develop expertise in a particular emerging technology, it becomes vital to understand the role that each of these technologies plays in the digital transformation pathway of firms, who also differ in their business contexts. For us, this will also help to better contextualize the transition of the Indian IT sector toward emerging technologies to meet the custom needs of their clients from different industry verticals and having different capacities. We provide below a brief overview of three of the key emerging technologies – IoT, Blockchain, and AI. We briefly discuss the value that these technologies might add to one or more activities in a firm's value chain, and how one

Table 3.1 Firm's value chain activities, context variables, and steps to transformation

Value chain activities related to a firm				
Inbound logistics	Production and Operations	Outbound logistics	Marketing and Sales	Service
Transactions with suppliers	Core activities taken up within firm	Transactions with wholesalers, retailers, end consumers		

Firm's context variables

1 Financial capacity: Access to investments, collaterals.
2 Knowledge constraints: Access to knowledge beyond their specific value chain.
3 Resource constraints: Supplier and consumer networks, Employee expertise.

Sequential steps toward digital transformation of core activities

1 Asset management: gather requisite data from production devices
2 Data governance: manage gathered data and build data analytics pipelines
3 Application management: information systems and applications to manipulate and manage production components
4 Process transformation: manage value chain activities associated with production and operations from cyberspace
5 Organizational alignment: align organizational strategy and human resource practices

may conceive of their customization possibilities depending on the present situation they are in. Although cloud is also an emerging technology, it relies more on the key principles underpinning software engineering and linked to the delivery of software solutions. Therefore, we discuss it in the subsequent section when dealing with the delivery of software solutions by IT service providers. Needless to say, for these organizations, both traditional software development and software development for cloud have mature workflows as compared to other emerging technologies like AI[17].

3.1.2.1 Internet of Things (IoT)

IoT is visualized as smart products, capable of relaying information about their status to the firm that then provides additional services to the end-users such as predictive maintenance based on insights gathered from such information. IoT enables advanced services not only in augmenting the product but also in improving the firm's value chain encompassing the entire product's lifecycle[18]. Physical components, either the product or the devices within a production system, are equipped with sensors, actuators, processors, and connection interfaces. These components are interconnected through inter-operable communication technologies and are managed either centrally or in a distributed manner with the help of software systems and applications built over them[19]. Functioning of various physical things or components can be manipulated and managed for improving different activities within a firm's value chain.

In their work on driving process innovation with IoT field data, Bilgeri et al.[20] illustrate the value added by IoT solutions in different activities of a firm's value chain by means of illustrative real-world cases. In the design and development activity, operational data relayed from prototype products help in better defining the product specifications and accelerating product validation. Actionable insights on the sensor-generated digital data streams during the production process can help in identifying root-cause of any errors and in optimizing and customizing production process. Increased reliability and efficiency of production process will also aid a better and cost-effective planning of inbound and outbound logistic activities. With regard to marketing and sales activity, the product usage data gathered from end customers will be useful to gain insights about customer behavior. This helps firms to identify different customer segments by their product preferences and to retain them by offering customized products and services. Enhanced service efficiency can be achieved by offering predictive maintenance solutions to customers based on the digital data streams communicated during their product usage.

Depending on the context of a firm and the maturity of its extant production processes, IoT solutions need to be conceived in stages[21]. For those at the beginning stages, it is important to automate data collection from their prototype products, associated production activities, and product usage trends. It is also essential to integrate support and service activities. Those at the intermediate level could enable data collection from end-user product usage and from production devices, in real time. Data analytics pipelines need to be built so as to gather insights from such data for enhancing production quality control, conducting customized marketing for individual users, and increasing automation within the support process. Those at the advanced level could build virtual digital twins giving cyber-level control over their physical production systems. This could also help them change product configuration settings for individual customers. Additionally, they could proactively offer product maintenance services and market complementary products/services based on individual customer needs.

3.1.2.2 *Blockchain*

Blockchain is a distributed digital ledger shared on a peer-to-peer network between members, some or all of whom can validate transactions between members following a predefined protocol. Such distributed ledgers can be permissioned, where members differ by their rights to participate in the network, centralized, where specific users are allocated with greater rights, or decentralized, where all users possess equal rights[22]. Digital records about the transactional activities carried out by a firm with internal or external stakeholders are a precondition for the incorporation of Blockchain as a technology. It can reduce the cost of transaction by facilitating trustworthy verification of transactional attributes like the stakeholders' credentials, features of product/service exchanged, etc., without the need for intermediaries.

Transacting stakeholders could be individuals, organizations, machines, or algorithms within smart contracts. Blockchain can facilitate trust, a role that is traditionally played by human agents in business[23].

Blockchain helps to enhance the level of information integration among entities within and beyond a firm's value chain. It increases the traceability and transparency about input resources or output products thereby formalizing the transactional relationships of a firm with its suppliers or customers. This adds value to the firm by reducing the risk and cost of product recalls. Bumblauskas et al.[24] richly illustrate the real-world case of a Blockchain use-case in food distribution. Blockchain here is implemented by a service provider to a client who specializes in egg processing and packing. Customized sensor networks were used to track and collect data on humidity and temperature levels at key points within the egg supply chain[25]. This helped in the creation of a digital record for each egg container. Blockchain helped in proving the origin, quality, authenticity, and compliance (in terms of humidity and temperature conditions that the eggs are subjected to) of every egg container that the client delivers to their downstream retail stores. This rich information is accessible to every stakeholder in the supply chain, which is a permissioned Blockchain network initiated by the client. Smart contracts in such example could be used to define and specify transaction fees and incentives to different stakeholders associated with production, processing, or consumption. Blockchain is also helpful to reduce the 'Bullwhip effect' – 'the observed propensity for material orders to be more variable than demand signals and for this variability to increase the further upstream a company is in a supply chain'[26] – in such supply chains with the help of accurate and traceable information sharing and smart contracts that prevent over-ordering[27].

In the example discussed above, illustrated by Bumblauskas et al., the service provider had to closely work with the client to build a solution that is feasible and compatible given the existing processes and infrastructure within the client's firm. This required an in-depth understanding about client's operations, performance requirements, privacy concerns, and the relevance of this solution in terms of the expected value addition to relevant stakeholders within and beyond the client's firm in their supply chain. Further, the activity of maintaining traceability data was largely standardized in the client's firm, which helped the service provider to digitalize such activity and build a Blockchain solution. Process standardization is therefore a necessary feasibility condition for the design, development, and successful operation of customized Blockchain solutions[28].

3.1.2.3 Artificial Intelligence (AI)

AI is perhaps the most discussed emerging technology and its rise in prominence owes heavily to the powerful advancements made in communication, networking, storage, and processing technologies. Another important factor has been the rapid advancements made in the development of numerous machine learning (ML) algorithms addressing a variety of problem contexts – in terms of the data volume, variety, availability, and the nature of analytics that is required[29]. While data and ML algorithms are vital to AI solutions, the most important element within an AI solution is the domain structure or the problem context. According to Taddy et al.[30], domain structure specific to a firm's use-case, allows for breaking of a complex problem into many prediction problems that can be solved using a combination of general-purpose ML algorithms. The metrics for success or failure of an AI solution are therefore heavily contingent on the firm's business context.

In the context of industry 4.0, IoT provides a foundation for building software systems that allow firms to manipulate and manage different production components, and Blockchain ensures traceability and transparency of their products in the supply chain. AI then leverages the foundational stacks facilitated by such technologies and helps firms to build the eventual customer-centric or process-enhancing applications promised by the former technologies. Applications around predictive maintenance of products or production components, inventory monitoring, process planning and control, etc. are all possible through the use of AI. Software engineering is a crucial requirement for building an AI solution, and so is the expertise around statistics and ML. However, the eventual value addition from adopting AI depends on how well such capabilities are utilized to make specific improvements to different value chain activities performed by the client firm.

A firm's extant process maturity is once again an important determinant of the kind of AI solution that could be possible. Bécue et al.[31] categorize AI solutions along *monitoring*, *optimization*, and *control*, depending on the level of maturity or progression of a firm's production process or value chain activities. A firm in its early stages of AI adoption can start by *monitoring* the performance of its systems and processes, by leveraging AI-based applications such as fault identification, preventive maintenance, and process quality control. ML models can be trained to learn the tacitly held knowledge of employees managing a firm's different value chain activities and the internal state of their complex production systems. Once these applications mature and garner the trust of a firm's stakeholders, it can move to the next stage, i.e., AI for *optimization*. Here the firm can enhance AI solutions further and build planning and decision support systems. Such systems can help in driving firm's activities toward meeting a desired set of business metrics. After sufficient maturity is realized at this stage, firms can then leverage AI to *control* different production activities and systems, to build customized products meeting individualized customer demands in a relatively short period of time. Moving from one stage to the next requires the firm to overcome several technical, operational, and security-related challenges. Technical challenges revolve around meeting the costs associated with data acquisition and storage, training ML models, and minimizing production or process disruptions. Operational challenges involve bearing the cost of specialized talent required to build AI solutions, their maintenance, compliance with regulatory requirements, and making the necessary trade-offs around the

Table 3.2 Summary of technologies

Technology	Value addition	Stages of development
Internet of Things	Interconnection of smart devices. Applications to manage their operation to improve value chain activities.	Data collection and analytics, to digital twin and self-organizable production systems.
Blockchain	Increases the traceability and transparency about input resources or output products and formalizes transactional relationships of a firm with its suppliers or customers.	Process maturity is a precondition for deploying Blockchain solutions.
Artificial Intelligence	Helps in realizing process improvement or customer-centric applications.	Address use-cases around process monitoring, followed by optimization, and then control.

cost of failure and change associated with the adoption of AI. Security is critical for many firms and the unpredictability of AI-based systems makes it highly challenging to address them as the firm evolves through increased adoption of AI. Table 3.2 provides a summary of the above discussion.

3.2 Delivering software vs emerging technology solutions

Outsourced software and business process services have been a traditional strong hold of service providers in the Indian IT sector. ITSO, for example, had an experience of around 30 years in this space. Companies like ITSO have already contributed significantly to the process evolution within client firms around their value chain activities. With a fair amount of this process maturity, clients are now positioned to deploy emerging technology solutions as well. Moreover, tremendous increases in the volume and variety of data generated from their business processes are necessitating the adoption of appropriate business intelligence solutions for them to remain competitive[32]. The Indian IT services organizations in general, and ITSO in particular, are witnessing a rising demand for emerging technology solutions from their long-standing clients. However, as we discussed in the previous section, delivering emerging technology solutions will require the service provider to consider a client firm's business context, its capabilities, and the maturity of processes associated with its present value chain activities. For that, they will have to negotiate appropriate workflows with their clients, which are different from their extant workflows of the traditional IT–BPM service delivery. Figure 3.1 summarizes this situation diagrammatically.

Before we dwell in the subsequent sections over the findings from our work ethnography in ITSO, we believe it is essential from a service provider's view to briefly cover the differences in software vs emerging technology solutions.

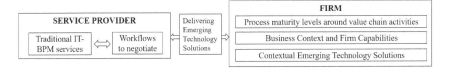

Figure 3.1 Providing emerging technology solutions to clients

In particular, we highlight the workflow-related differences between these two with a greater focus on AI solutions, as they are the mainstay for ITSO's AI research lab – our ethnographic site.

3.2.1 Delivering software solutions

3.2.1.1 Principles guiding software development

According to Ghezzi et al.[33], software development and software workflows are guided by a set of general principles – Rigor and formality, separation of concerns, modularity, abstraction, anticipation of change, generality, and incrementality. *Rigor and formality* define the precision and exactness of software products and processes, often evaluated by mathematical laws. *Separation of concerns* helps to divide a problem along different aspects and tackle each of them individually. It could be manifested through the separation of development activities across time, of technical and managerial tasks in the development process, of use-case-related concerns and the implementation-related concerns, etc. *Modularity* drives a division of complex system into smaller modules or a composition of a complex system from existing modules. It allows for separation of concerns in terms of dealing with the details of a given module in isolation and of the integration of different modules into an integrated system. *Abstraction* is also a form of separation of concerns where the high-level use-case-related services and features are separated from their detailed implementation-level programs/codes. *Anticipation of change* is required in software development as the requirements are not fully understood at any given point in time. It often forms the basis for deciding upon modularization strategy. Anticipating future requirements enables incorporation of additional elements into software system design thereby making it evolvable effectively in the future. It also affects the reusability of software components and helps managers to make trade-offs in terms of the time and effort to spend in the development of reusable components. *Generality* is another fundamental principle that allows software teams to develop general tools or packages anticipating their potential usage. Off-the-shelf packages which have become a general trend in software are one result of this principle. Since software requirements are not stable or fully understood at any given point, *incrementality* principle is vital for developers to build subsets of an application for early customer feedback. This helps in the evolution of software in a controllable manner.

The workflow or life-cycle of software development entails four major activities[34]. First is the requirements analysis, where the requirements expected from the software for a specific use-case are elicited and analyzed for their feasibility in terms of costs and benefits. Second is the architectural design which entails a high-level organization of the software system in terms of the abstract modules and their interactions. Third is the detailed design which provides increasingly detailed information about individual modules and their precisely defined interfaces. Fourth is the implementation where actual codes produced by engineers are integrated and composed as a running system to be delivered to the customer. These aforementioned principles guide the development activities and also their organization within the overarching workflow adopted by the service provider for a given use-case. In the traditional waterfall-based approach, these activities are separated and carried out sequentially, while in case of agile there is a provision for iteration between these activities to facilitate incremental development[35]. Tasks within each of these activities are also separated and assigned to different work roles. For example, a business analyst usually engages in the activities concerning requirements analysis and architectural design and prepares high-level architectural diagrams or frameworks for a given use-case based on the requirements elicited from the customer. These high-level architectural designs help software architects to build detailed design. In this activity, the architect follows the principles of modularity and abstraction and composes the complex software system in terms of abstract modules and their interfaces. The detailed design guides software engineers to write codes for their respective modules independently, and then integrate them as a complete system. The aforementioned principles are also the basis for different methods, techniques, methodologies, and tools that are adopted in the process of software development. Methods and techniques provide guidelines governing the execution of different activities in the software life-cycle, and they are often packaged together as methodologies. Tools are built to support the application of different methodologies.

3.2.1.2 Software development for Cloud

A major issue with traditional software systems built for deployment in client's on-premise servers is that of their scalability. Limitations related to the available infrastructure make the client's software difficult to scale when the need arises to make it available for rapidly adding new customers. It is on this issue of scalability where software development in cloud wins over traditional software development with deployment done on on-premise servers. According to the definition[36] provided by the National Institute of Standards and Technology (NIST), the services offered by cloud are considered at three levels depending on the nature of IT operations –concerns with the day-to-day provision of IT services to customers, rather than the development of software. Under Infrastructure-as-a-Service (IaaS), infrastructure resources, such as computing power, networking, and storage, are dynamically provisioned by cloud service provider on-demand to the customers – who either build platforms or software applications. In this model, customers will need to define the infrastructure to be provisioned and then completely focus on managing their platforms or software. Physical management of such provisioned infrastructure is completely taken care of by the cloud provider. Under Platform-as-a-Service (PaaS), the cloud service providers offer the complete platform to the customers where they could build and run applications directly without worrying about any infrastructure provisioning. Cloud provider takes care of auto-scaling platform resources so that the customer's application can cater to any increase in the number of its users. Under Software-as-a-Service (SaaS), software applications are directly provided by the service providers and end customers are the only users of such applications. As can be seen, each kind of service increasingly abstracts out the operational tasks associated with a software application and makes it easy for the end customers, in particular for the developers[37].

Methodology, such as DevOps, an evolution of agile, is gaining immense popularity in the context of organizing software development activities for cloud. Software development and the organization of associated activities under this new methodology are also guided by the same set of principles discussed previously[38]. DevOps signifies the combination of activities associated with software development and IT operations. Following the incrementality principle, it advocates for incremental delivery of software versions in much shorter cycles, or continuous delivery, while ensuring their correctness and reliability[39]. To achieve continuous delivery, software development for Cloud also relies on microservices architecture where the architectural design of software is composed of 'independently deployable units' called microservices[40]. Separation of concerns is seen in terms of each microservice built to achieve a specific business capability and interacts with other services through the network[41]. Software development for Cloud is also subjected to additional restrictions in terms of the abstraction of operational technicalities that the developers in PaaS or IaaS will work with. Such restrictions enforce strict adherence to the principles of software engineering and foster best practices that ensure fault tolerance and scalability of software[42].

3.2.2 *Comparison with emerging technologies*

Clients across the globe are attracted to the Indian IT services companies for their mature process workflows in the development and delivery of client-centric software solutions. Mature workflows help with a clear division of work between various roles, which is again important for service providers to reliably budget their human resources for client projects. While the workflows are mature in case of software development, same is not true in case of emerging technology solutions. We highlight some characteristic differences between activities, workflows, and work role assignments, associated with emerging technology solutions vs software development. We particularly focus on AI vs software development, and wherever relevant discuss the similarities of AI with other emerging technologies in these aspects.

3.2.2.1 *Maturity of development workflows*

As discussed earlier, a firm's business context and the domain knowledge specific to such a context drive the data management and ML modeling strategies in the context of building AI solutions. Software solutions also depend on the firm's context, but their standardized development workflows are built on principles that separate the concerns between activities, depending on the firm's business context such as the requirements elicitation vs the detailed software design and programming aspects. Difference between developing software and AI solutions is clearly articulated by Amershi et al.[43] who described AI development as being highly data and use-case centric, unlike software development that is centered around modules of software and the software architectural design. Sculley et al.[44] describe in detail the incompatibility of a key software development principle, that of modularity while dealing with two major activities in the case of AI – data preprocessing and ML model building. These activities are so entangled and connected intricately with the use-case that even a slightest update in the use-case requirement can completely change the data preprocessing and ML modeling activities. Abstraction boundaries are also relatively difficult to envisage in case of AI development. While anticipation of change is important, reusing previously developed work components is less possible owing to the fact that it is difficult to handle AI work components as distinct modules. For organizations known for their standardized service delivery workflows around software development, a move toward providing AI solutions, therefore, requires a rather revolutionary adjustment of workflows.

3.2.2.2 *Work roles straddling between activities*

Absence of strict abstraction boundaries between different components in an AI solution makes the division of work between different roles relatively more difficult compared to traditional software development. Constant iterative interaction between work roles handling different development activities is mandatory for building AI solutions optimal for a client's particular use-case[45]. In software development, separation of concerns manifests in the form of a clear division of tasks between managerial and technical roles for a given project. For example, the requirement analysis is typically carried out by a business analyst, detailed architectural design is handled by a software architect, and coding of independent modules in isolation is carried out by respective software engineers[46]. However, domain knowledge pertaining to a firm's specific AI use-case becomes paramount for developers working with their general-purpose tools or platforms[47]. Data scientists are a good example of such developers who are expected to have expertise in drawing domain-related structure of a firm, along with practice of software engineering, and theoretical depth of ML [48]. As we discussed earlier, evolutionary stages of emerging technology solutions development depend upon a firm's process maturity. Such solutions are often realized by a synergy of other technologies making standardization of workflows a complex endeavor and therefore rather difficult. For example, solutions for industry 4.0 are realized by the synergy of emerging communication, control, and computing technology solutions tailor-made for specific technical/business context of a firm[49]. Even if standardized for a particular set of use-cases within the industry, or for firms reaching a certain level of maturity, the workflows still may not allow clear separation of work activities between different roles, on par with software development. This peculiar aspect in the context of AI solution development is highlighted by researchers working toward the standardization of AI workflows[50].

3.3 Client-centric AI solutions by ITSO's research lab

We now come to our specific ethnographic study site, the AI research lab of ITSO, which has been delivering AI offerings to clients, largely based on augmenting their existing, traditional IT and BPM services. Projects based on Natural Language Processing (NLP), a sub-domain within ML – an important technological element within AI – dominated such offerings. Other sub-domains within ML like Computer Vision, Speech Processing, Graph Machine Learning, and so on, and other technologies, like Blockchain, IoT, Quantum Computing, and so on, were dealt with more as ongoing research agenda set by the team lead for this research lab.

We draw inferences about the workflows and role assignments in the context of AI project within this lab, through our active participation in the NLP project in which the ethnographer worked with other members of the lab.

3.3.1 The ethnographer's project in the AI research lab

The work ethnography in the AI research lab at ITSO helped us to uncover the complexities of work and work interactions in complex AI-related projects. The AI project in which the ethnographer worked involved automation around the extraction of a specific set of fields from legal documents of clients. Until now, the BPM teams in the organization had to process such documents by manually searching for such fields and entering them into the client's database. Such documents ran into several thousand each month. A recent legislation in the EU mandating the digitalization of such documents increased the significance of this for the clients. Since this was not among their core activities, it made sense for them to offshore such work to their extant service providers, like this organization. The automation use-case in this regard was expected to reduce costs by having these activities done with

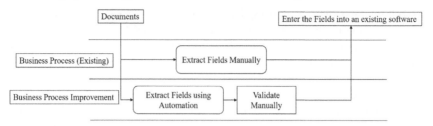

Figure 3.2 NLP use-case

relatively less manual intervention. Some level of manual intervention still continues because of the inherent limitations of AI, which makes manual validation and correction of AI output, mandatory. Figure 3.2 diagrammatically represents this business use-case.

Data preprocessing and ML model building are the two major implementation-related activities that warrant elaboration. These activities are central to the AI solutions worked on by the technical roles – the data engineers and data scientists. For the current NLP project, Harish, Vinod, and the ethnographer were the data engineers and Sruthi was the data scientist. While the former engaged with data preprocessing tasks, the latter was responsible for model-building activity. Below we summarize these activities based on the observations and field notes of the ethnographer, working with these able team members.

Data preprocessing involves extraction of the entire corpus of the text from each document, segmenting of the text corpus into tokens, which could be paragraphs/sentences/words, and subsequently representing every token through a set of numeric features (x). Standard NLP packages such as 'NLTK' and 'spaCy' in Python are used to extract tokens, features, and structure the data in a tabular format – in the form of a data-frame object. Within this data-frame, tokens corresponding to the to-be extracted fields are manually labeled (y) and the updated data-frame is ready to be fed into subsequent activity – that is model training-cum-evaluation. Model training-cum-evaluation involved trying out various supervising learning models, starting with very basic models such as Logistic Regression to the most advanced ones such as Sequence Models. This second activity is taken up by the data scientists who apply their theoretical understanding to justify selection of appropriate ML models for the given business use-case.

AI projects are centered around data, and preprocessing of the data is the most time taking aspect during implementation. Data comes with a particular type and format depending on the client's business use-case. In one of their previous projects related to a sales forecasting use-case, the client data was properly structured in a tabular format (referred to as a 'data-frame') with rows capturing observations of a particular month's supply parameters, all in numeric data types. Numeric type data-frames are directly amenable to performing the ML model-building activity. In cases where the business use-case revolves around extracting inferences from documents, such as text summarization, extraction of key fields, sentiment analysis, and so on, the type of the data is not numeric but text, and the data is available in the format of a document (e.g., .pdf). Data can also be images, videos, speech, and so on, and structure of the data accordingly determines the format in which it is stored (e.g., .jpg for image, .mp4 for video, .mp3 for speech). Data from IoT sensors in industry 4.0 use-cases come in the form of electric voltage signals representing various environmental variables such as temperature, pressure, humidity, etc. In these latter types of data, a lot of preprocessing effort will be required to bring the data into numeric type and structure them into data-frames suitable for ML model building. For the current NLP project that we worked on, the data type was text and was presented in the form of documents. Structuring this data required extraction of tokens (e.g., sentences) and corresponding features (e.g., vector capturing frequency of different words in a sentence).

ML model building is an important technological element in AI projects and the appropriate strategy for it depends upon the client's specific business use-case. The universe of ML models is commonly divided into supervised, unsupervised, and reinforcement models[51]. Supervised learning models are function approximation problems where the training data are a collection of (x, y) pairs (x – feature vector, y – response/label) and the goal is to produce a prediction y* in response to a query x*. Unsupervised learning models are exploratory data analysis models that involve the analysis of unlabeled data for drawing inferences about whether the data has any latent structure that can be extracted. Lastly, reinforcement learning models are trained in settings where a system needs to arrive at an optimal policy for action within an environment while maximizing its expected reward or success. A majority of the projects undertaken by the AI team at ITSO dealt with supervised and unsupervised learning models. While data availability in a standard type and format is necessary for enabling model development, the relevance of features captured within the data contributes to the overall performance of ML models for a given use-case[52]. In addition, theoretical understanding of when and what ML models should be experimented with for a given use-case is a must for individuals engaged with model-building tasks.

Software platforms are vital for AI projects as they help the technical roles with the necessary tools and packages to write programs for preprocessing and ML model building. Python and R are the common programming platforms used by the members of this team. In the context of an AI project, these platforms enable members to write programs for preprocessing data and run ML models using off-the-shelf packages that are developed by the respective platform-specific open-source communities. While the most used and stable packages are available for installing from the integrated development environments (IDEs) corresponding to each of the platforms (e.g., Spyder IDE and jupyter notebook are commonly used by the team for Python and R-studio IDE is used in case of R), packages covering advanced and cutting-edge ML models are usually downloaded from online open-source repositories such as GitHub. These programming platforms also enable individuals to develop traditional software programs. Particularly for data preprocessing tasks, it enables team members to work on rule-based software programs essential for extracting tokens and features from unstructured text documents. Programming platforms also allow the members to deploy their final AI solutions either standalone or integrated with some customer software onto cloud platforms (such as Microsoft Azure, Amazon Web Services – AWS, Google Cloud Platform – GCP) or even onto the client's on-premise servers.

3.3.2 Workflows negotiated for AI projects

Based on the work in the NLP project and conversations with lab-mates, the ethnographer was able to identify the following implementation activities within an overarching workflow that the lab negotiated for developing and delivering AI projects to its clients. We discuss below, the various stages of this tentative, negotiated workflow carved out in ITSO's AI research lab.

3.3.2.1 Use-case identification

A majority of AI projects undertaken by this lab serve the purpose of augmenting the existing IT-BPM solutions that this organization has been delivering to its clients. The AI research lab's team lead joins the sales team of this organization in client-service provider negotiations meant for its usual IT-BPM projects. Any proposal for cost-reduction through AI that comes up during such negotiations is immediately analyzed in terms of the total resource costs and value propositions that it offers to the AI research lab and the organization. Business analysts are engaged for evaluating in-house expertise of their members as well as the prospective value that could be generated by taking up such a project. Once decided, the team lead arranges a visit to the client site with a group comprising the project manager, business analyst, and a data scientist. Spending time at the client site, such a group works to map the client business requirements into AI use-cases. At this stage, both the business analyst and project manager jointly mediate communication between data scientists and clients' business team and ensure that the use-cases are mapped for client's requirements in a short time, in a workshop mode. The data scientist brings her prior experience from previous projects in terms of the applicability of various ML models to client's requirements and estimates the manpower and resources required to process the pertinent data to train these models. At the end of this stage, the business analyst and the project manager together prepare high-level diagrams for each of the client use-cases, which also capture the strategies for reusing components from previous projects and wherever required, the need to develop new ones. For the current NLP project, Kamal was the business analyst as well as project manager, depending on the stage of the project, and Sruthi was picked up as the data scientist.

3.3.2.2 Proof of concept

If the use-cases are novel, data scientists work on building proof of concept (POC) ML models based on off-the-shelf data, closely resembling the nature of client data. In such projects, data scientists regularly engage with clients to agree upon key performance indicators (KPIs) and also exchange domain knowledge underpinning client's use-case. Although they conceive appropriate preprocessing strategies to extract pertinent features from data given the use-case, they largely stick to off-the-shelf data available from previous projects that are readily amenable for model-building activity. They prefer engaging formally during POC stages of the project because it gives them a chance to develop IP cores and meet the research expectations set by the team lead for this team. As Sruthi put it, *"we don't want those kinds of projects which don't have ideation time. There should be something for us also, to build small IPs. Although we might get thoughts from the client but eventually for reuse or scalability, we have to build small IPs."* IP cores developed during these POCs or otherwise are important for the team, as the team lead prefers to utilize these IPs not just for pitching customizable AI solutions to clients but also reuse them while executing future client projects. One of our key observations was that during POC stages, the data scientists often have to go through 'agile sprints' – a practice typically followed during software development projects within this organization, to provide incremental status updates to clients. We have seen in section above, how AI workflows don't allow for incremental updates as in traditional software projects. The data scientists, therefore, have to smartly negotiate to get their required inputs for building POCs during these sprints. In this regard, Sruthi talked about her experience from one of her previous projects as to how they managed such sprints,

> *He [the business person from client's side] doesn't understand the tech complexity. Still, we have to give weekly [updates] in sprints [agile sprints]. Our understanding should match with the clients' understanding. So, we devised a dashboard for helping clients to give us inputs. How they drilled down the dashboard and all, gave us indirect cues and feedback for us to build models. They may say "these things will not impact, those will", which gives us factors [for pre-processing stage]. What we were creating was an analytics framework and they were giving us the meat. We iteratively showed them some results with addition of new features [similar to incremental progress update in traditional software development].*

3.3.2.3 Execution and deployment

For most client use-cases, the project directly proceeds to execution stage skipping the POC stage. In this execution stage, data engineers engage with the development of preprocessing programs as we discussed earlier. During the initial period of the execution stage, data scientists interact informally with data engineers and guide them to undertake preprocessing efforts, keeping in mind the prospective client data and available IP cores. Efforts of the data engineers are supervised, formally, during project status meetings held by business analysts, project managers, and the team lead; mainly along the lines of their implementation of high-level customization and reuse strategies that business analysts had come up with. We observed that, across projects, the interaction between data engineers and data scientists tapers off beyond this initial period of the execution stage. According to Kamal, this is because *"the hourly billing rate for data scientists is very high in comparison to data engineers"*. After preprocessing programs are developed by data engineers over a preliminary set of client data, software/cloud engineers integrate them with closely compatible ML models from previous projects and deploy this as a complete AI solution over Cloud. Here, the cloud architect takes an architecture-centric approach treating the preprocessing programs and selected ML models as modules and drives their integration along the high-level frameworks prepared by the business analyst. For the current project, Yuvraj was the cloud architect, and Sameer and Javed were the software/cloud engineers. This architecture-centric approach allows the cloud architect to make reliable estimates about the usage of costly cloud computing resources in a given project. Software/cloud engineers create appropriate web-based user interfaces for clients to access this resulting AI solution as a service and to expose their full volume and variety of data. This ex-post exposing of full client data to the AI solution creates several issues making work difficult for data engineers. Krishna, one of the data scientists working on another project, describes these problems as follows,

> *I think it is a bad idea to club front-end Dev [Building interfaces for clients] and ML Dev. There should be two different plans to get into this. While they [client's databases] were up and running, we had problems. We had to push doc [documents] to other place, fetch and pull resources so on. We had to always deal with [managing] proper versions of docs, meta-data and so on that the front-end teams and client-side teams were using. Eventually we had to convince them [for letting us work] with dummy data. There was lot of unnecessary rework and overhead.*

Such problems are an offshoot of not working on the full client-data right from the beginning as expected in an ideal-typical AI execution – where full volume and variety of data drives iterative experimentation between preprocessing and ML model-building activities to arrive at optimal AI solution[53].

3.3.2.4 Post deployment

Data scientists once again engage in the project after deployment, when the final AI solution is exposed to the full volume and variety of client-data. Here again, data scientists only play an advisory role. Data engineers are responsible for enhancing preprocessing programs and integrating appropriate ML models for improving performance toward the agreed upon KPIs.

This post-deployment stage formally engages data engineers and software/ cloud engineers, and periodic status about improvements has to be reported to clients through 'agile sprints'. According to the members of the lab, agile sprints are constituted mainly by periodic meetings between clients and service providers to ensure incremental development of software while incorporating dynamic requirements from clients. However, they fail to appreciate their use during AI projects. Based on experience from a previous project, Krishna had this to say, "*In ML sense, giving updates daily [or weekly] makes no sense, what will you say? I did this experiment and got this result? You can't update like that. But still we did that. Just because it's a SW engineering practice.*" In addition to AI work components, depending on the requirement, software/cloud engineers are also required to build UIs for clients to access AI solutions and expose their full data, again within the routine decided by these agile sprints.

3.3.3 Dominance of software engineering principles

Activities pertaining to a given AI use-case will contribute toward building an optimal solution only when they are organized around the use-case and the corresponding data[54]. From the foregoing discussion, we see that in ITSO, activities related to project implementation, such as the preprocessing and model building, are guided predominantly by the principles of software development. Separation of concerns akin to software development is clearly seen by the manner in which the managerial roles were detached from the substantive work taken up by the data engineers, beyond oversight during project status meetings. They also anticipated changes in the AI projects to be undertaken along the lines of software development. The preprocessing and ML models were treated as isolated modules and with high customizability and reusability, conducive to high-level software frameworks. Even among the technical roles – data scientists, data engineers, cloud architects, cloud engineers – separation of their work responsibilities along different activities were clearly charted. Data engineers worked mainly on preprocessing, cloud engineers on deployment, data scientists on model building, and cloud architects on guiding the deployment along a high-level framework. Modularity of preprocessing programs and ML models, and their reuse from previous projects, was tacitly assumed and the abstractions around them underpinned the high-level frameworks built during use-case identification or followed during deployment. Incremental development was a norm even during prototype stages, in contrast to its incompatibility in the context of AI solution development as the data engineers of the team argued, and as the literature also speaks about[55].

Data scientists predominantly engaged with off-the-shelf data and experimented with advanced ML models and strategies. An important work taken up by data scientists is to streamline end-to-end workflows within AI projects. We noticed that they were experimenting with an open-source ML workflow called ML Flow. This new workflow helps to keep track of inputs to an AI solution (such as data-versions, preprocessing programs, and ML model parameters), reproduce results, and ensure relatively time-efficient experimentation post-deployment[56]. The team lead hopes to mandate this new workflow for most of the AI projects to be taken up in the future. Adopting such a workflow will offer a better context about work in a particular activity performed by different technical roles and will also allow transitioning from the current negotiated workflows, incompatible with such roles during AI solution development. Data scientists were initiating meetings with the leading clients of this organization to make them aware of the scope for incorporation of such workflows, but to what extent will they materialize is still to be seen.

3.4 Challenges in the transition toward emerging technologies

In the first section of this chapter, we looked at the importance of a firm's business context and the maturity of its processes for reaping value out of emerging technology solutions. Building on this, we then discussed from the IT services provider perspective, how and why delivering software solutions are characteristically different from delivering emerging technology solutions. We highlighted the incompatibility of some of the software engineering principles when applied to the development of emerging technology solutions. We also highlighted some key differences between developing software and emerging technology solutions in terms of the maturity of development workflows and the possible separation of work between different roles. We then specifically looked at the AI project undertaken by an Indian IT services organization. Here, we illustrated details about the AI-specific activities, and the way they were negotiated within workflows largely underpinned by software engineering principles and relatively incompatible with the development of use-case optimal AI solutions. We now highlight the challenges these workflows pose, to ITSO's transition into the emerging technology space.

3.4.1 Servicing lower end in the client's value chain

From providing simple software and business process services to now offering customized emerging technology solutions, IT services companies in India have moved up a long way in terms of the value they contribute to client's business activities. They have made tremendous advancements in terms of improving their service delivery workflows and attained highest maturity levels globally. Emerging technology solutions, particularly around AI, are expected to provide both, high-value services to clients around maximizing their production and operational efficiencies and also relatively low-value services around marketing, sales, and service. Our illustration of a typical AI project taken up by the IT services organization tells us that for the

Indian IT sector, such projects are situated at a relatively lower end in the client's business value chain. Firstly, these projects are not aiming to tackle the process improvements of the client's core value chain activities – production and operations. Instead, a majority of them, since they are 'augmented' services meant to support client's non-core value chain activities – such as their customer interaction activities like marketing, sales, and support[57] only add incremental value to their existing IT-BPM services.

Emerging technology solutions for servicing this relatively lower-end of client's value chain is believed to be remunerative for the lab according to some of its members, and as we saw the lab is actively involved in sourcing such projects from existing clients. Despite the lab's avowed goal of garnering expertise in AI, the implicit yet influential mandate of working on client-centric AI projects is a necessary responsibility for this lab to avoid it becoming a cost center within the company. As the team lead states, '*team with 35 odd people is a cost centre for the company … so our investment into IPs has to show some results for clients … if not the management might place us back into consulting*'. The lab and its members argue that serving this lower end of client's value chain through their AI projects will be a crucial competitive edge for IT services companies when compared to other product-based AI companies. In this regard, Sruthi says that '*companies like Google are streamlining their [client-centric] workflows to deliver customized AI solutions, a space in which they were not there before … but we have a competitive edge here given our primary focus has always been to deliver customized solutions to clients from the beginning.*' The team lead also believes that AI augmenting IT-BPM services is perhaps the only plausible way for IT services companies in India to reach scale in terms of revenues. In one of the discussions with the ethnographer, he argues in favor of such augmented services and says, "*the kind of project we talked about [current AI project] … such a huge client-based project will be impossible for companies that wish to work on standalone AI projects. Typical ones run into few thousand dollars but not into millions. Bundling with other services and selling integrated solutions will fetch good revenues.*"[58]

The workflows that this lab has negotiated with clients for AI projects reinforce this reality of ITSO's emerging technology work targeting the relatively lower end of the client's value chain. AI workflows continue to be largely underpinned by a dominance of software engineering principles and are largely reminiscent of the standard service delivery workflows adopted by this organization for its mainstream IT-BPM services. Client-driven incremental delivery-related sprints during almost every stage in the AI project bear one evidence of this. Clients too have settled for such workflows, because they help in getting reliable estimates from service providers about the manpower, time, and other resources dedicated to a particular project. But these workflows prevent the IT services organization in venturing higher-up the client's value chain in the context of the latter's digital transformation goals. For example, the separation of technical and managerial activities, as observed during the execution of a project, isolates the technical roles, mainly the data engineers, from having a substantive engagement with the client's business use-case. Data scientists face clients during prototype stages and are in position to build models considering the domain structure of a client's business use-case, but the separation of AI preprocessing from model building, dilutes the extent to which domain structure guides their activities and affects the use-case optimality of the resulting solutions. Client-side limitations in terms of a lack of data management infrastructure, data sharing concerns, etc. are also other bottlenecks for the AI research lab to support the core activities of the clients.

Anticipating future projects aimed at the higher end of client's value chain – like adding value to client's core production and operations – are still driven by research agendas of the individual data scientists. Majority of the IP cores of this lab are a result of concepts built in augmenting IT-BPM services through AI solutions for different clients. These IP cores are important for the lab in deriving their value internally during sales pitches, but this outlook prevents the IT services organizations from scaling up the value chain. As discussed in the beginning sections, to make a substantive mark in the emerging technology space will require service providers to take an evolutionary approach to building solutions. Such solutions will be contingent upon the current maturity level in processes associated with client's value chain activities. Therefore, to build such solutions it becomes imperative for organizations like ITSO to renegotiate their workflows differently for emerging technology projects. However, according to Yuvraj, the cloud architect, the dominance of ITSO's long-standing clients, and the separation of technical and managerial roles hinder this process. With regard to the latter, he says, "*Business analysts have a broad-brush understanding of the AI solutions that are developed in-house by data-scientists or engineers. They flamboyantly decorate this understanding [for clients]. But it is the data-scientists and data-engineers who will know better which AI solutions will work where since they are aware of their theoretical underpinnings.*" He compares service-based IT organizations with product-based ones highlighting the influence of clients in the process of negotiating work, "*In product-based companies, they bring all the employees on board for their own organization. Workflows and process[es] are streamlined for the betterment of the organization ... However, in service-based companies, especially when very big clients are at the center, things change. Whatever they [clients/customers] ask you must do ... this degrades the culture ... it doesn't allow the organization to build its own processes properly*"[59].

3.4.2 Difficulty in scaling-up the AI value chain

In the AI value chain, the main theme of discussion seen among the employees of this lab is around delivering generic AI products vs AI augmented with IT-BPM services. The former is regarded as having a higher value compared to the latter. Yuvraj, believes, "*service-based companies play it safe [as they engage] in low-end work in managing clients' non-core business processes ... greater value is added by product-based companies who build generic products.*" We observed that the lab relied heavily on generic platforms and tools developed by global software giants like Google, Microsoft, IBM, etc.[60], while offering tailor-made AI solutions for clients. These software giants had a first-mover advantage over the Indian IT sector in this space, and it is hard to move away from such a dependence on their platforms. No doubt, they are also leaps ahead in the space of Cloud, which again is vital to the deployment of AI solutions. But a sheer comparison of the emerging technology workforce shows that the IT services companies in India have close to 2,30,000 employees – way more than the 90,000 odd working in the prominent global giants[61]. With a far greater talent pool, there is a lot of scope for the IT services organizations to move up the AI value chain and also dominate generic product offerings in the space of AI.

The predicament facing these organizations is the reliance on existing clients for AI projects bundled with their IT-BPM solutions, which restricts the scope of going up the AI value chain through product offerings. The technical workforce in the emerging technology projects is overwhelmed by client demands through the peculiar client-convenient negotiated workflows, as we discussed above. This stymies innovation in the emerging technology space thus foreclosing the development of use-case optimal solutions. Client-side limitations in terms of a lack of data management infrastructure, data sharing concerns, etc., and their preferences for explainable and interpretable ML models further exacerbated the scope for innovation in the space of AI. As Sruthi, the data scientist, put it, "*[the] client was more comfortable with traditional statistical models … when we suggested deep learning … quoting explanation concerns he said no … we were getting 20% more accuracy with deep learning … but interpretability and explain-ability was more key so they were reluctant*". Data scientists who were spearheading research efforts also had come to believe that they should not be spending more time on building such advanced models, as it will only add to the lab's costs. Sruthi again, "*if we take time building advanced models by conducting research rigorously, then it may unnecessarily add to more costs, and also create more confusion to the clients, which we then have to clarify … so, in most of our work we do whatever possible to meet the client requirements, not more nor less … this doesn't give us any time to work out things in a proper manner, build systems that we could enhance through time …*"

3.4.3 Unplanned WFH that exacerbated challenges

An unplanned imposition of Work from Home (WFH), owing to the COVID-19 pandemic-imposed lockdown, also highlighted additional challenges in the Indian IT services organizations. In the initial period, there were visible concerns around security and infrastructure limitations that made it hard for IT services organizations to facilitate their employees working from home[62]. For established Big-Tech companies known for their general-purpose IT and emerging technology platforms, transition to

WFH was less difficult[63] as their processes were relatively less influenced by the wide array of customers they deal with. The situation was different for the IT services organizations. Although WFH authorizations were given to some teams at ITSO, including the members of the AI research lab, similar authorizations to other units seemed difficult. Concerns were expressed about breach of service agreements made with their clients in case IT–BPM work has to shift from secure office environments to home. However, the senior executives at ITSO also sent many reassuring emails to the employees, including the ethnographer, which presented a rosy picture about the possible growth prospects that might open up as clients will now accelerate their digital transformation. The ethnographer paraphrases from his/her recollection, the essence of one such mail as follows

> This is the time to go more client centric, transform workflows to move closer to clients, and partner with them in this difficult situation. It is an occasion and an opportunity for strengthening client-vendor relationships much more … this organization is proud of and is known for its customer centric approach and will continue to uphold it during these tough times … current pandemic situation will only accelerate the clients' need for modernization or digital transformation … it is the right time for this organization to virtualize everything they do, and they have enough abilities to do it right now.

While the transition to WFH was operationally less difficult for the AI research lab, it made the coordination between team members around the AI project work more challenging. The lab already had greater flexibility in terms of open Internet access and flexible work hours compared to other units/teams at ITSO. So, the operational difficulties were conspicuously absent. In fact, the team lead urged the members of this lab to pave a path for other teams by effectively moving their status meetings, workshops, and whiteboard discussions online. The challenge however was that the informal channels of communication built by the members of this lab to work around the incompatibilities associated with the current AI project workflows got diluted[64]. The workarounds that were informally negotiated in the premises of the research lab could no longer be accessed. These informal channels went beyond gaining tacit knowledge from teammates through discussions and conversations or water-cooler talks. They stemmed from the still tenuous nature of their AI project workflows and were critical for data engineers to obtain relevant technical and business context about the AI project from data scientists and business analysts. Atomistic team–members working from home on modular pieces of the project are still conceivable in software projects, but not so in AI projects, as we saw above. Software platforms for distributed teamwork such as virtual meeting and chat platforms streamlined the formal communication channels like the project status meetings. But they were ineffective in facilitating informal conversations during coffee breaks, lunch hours, etc., that were immensely significant for any exchange of ideas or information between employees.

Distributed teamwork is the norm in the context of software development where the standardized workflows provide greater scope for clear separation of work activities between members[65]. In the context of ITSO's AI research lab, the workflows that were negotiated with clients resembled software workflows and expected clear separation of work activities between members. But, in AI projects where all the development activities are centered around client's business use-case, technical and business context pertaining to such a use-case becomes far more important, and the WFH only exacerbated this challenge. Recent developments in the industry to build AI-compatible workflows[66] and similar developments that data scientists are driving in the ITSO's AI research lab are a first step in the direction of offering context appropriately to all the work roles engaging in an AI project. But, given the relative nascency of these new workflows and the difficulty of renegotiating with influential clients makes this transition a challenge for the Indian IT services organizations like ITSO.

Notes

1 Dopico, M., Gómez, A., De la Fuente, D., García, N., Rosillo, R., & Puche, J. (2016). A vision of industry 4.0 from an artificial intelligence point of view. Proceedings on the International Conference on Artificial Intelligence (ICAI), 407.
2 Xu, H., Yu, W., Griffith, D., & Golmie, N. (2018). A survey on industrial Internet of Things: A cyber-physical systems perspective. IEEE Access, 6, 78238–78259.
3 Bécue, A., Praça, I., & Gama, J. (2021). Artificial intelligence, cyber-threats and Industry 4.0: Challenges and opportunities. Artificial Intelligence Review, 54(5), 3849–3886.
4 Amershi, S., Begel, A., Bird, C., DeLine, R., Gall, H., Kamar, E., … Zimmermann, T. (2019). Software engineering for machine learning: A case study. 2019 IEEE/ACM 41st International Conference on Software Engineering: Software Engineering in Practice (ICSE-SEIP), 291–300. IEEE.
5 Davenport, T. H., & Patil, D. J. (2012). Data Scientist in the context of AI is one example of such a role who requires expertise at the intersection of machine learning, programming, and business domain knowledge. Data scientist. Harvard Business Review, 90(5), 70–76.
6 Taddy, M. (2019). Importance of domain expertise in the case of AI, a central technology underpinning industry 4.0, is highlighted. in: The technological elements of artificial intelligence. University of Chicago Press, Chicago, IL.
7 Dopico, M., Gómez, A., De la Fuente, D., García, N., Rosillo, R., & Puche, J. (2016). A vision of industry 4.0 from an artificial intelligence point of view. Proceedings on the International Conference on Artificial Intelligence (ICAI), 407.
8 Lasi, H., Fettke, P., Kemper, H.-G., Feld, T., & Hoffmann, M. (2014). Industry 4.0. Business & Information Systems Engineering, 6(4), 239–242.
9 According to Porter (1985) on competitive advantage, value chain of a firm comprises primary activities such as inbound logistics, operations, outbound logistics, marketing and sales, and service.
10 Jasra, J., Hunjra, A. I., Rehman, A. U., Azam, R. I., & Khan, M. A. (2011). Determinants of business success of small and medium enterprises. International Journal of Business and Social Science, 2(20).

11 Singh, R. K., Garg, S. K., Deshmukh, S. G., & Kumar, M. (2007). Modelling of critical success factors for implementation of AMTs. Journal of Modelling in Management.

12 Lee, S., Park, G., Yoon, B., & Park, J. (2010). Open innovation in SMEs—An intermediated network model. Research Policy, 39(2), 290–300.

13 Blind, K., & Mangelsdorf, A. (2012). Alliance formation of SMEs: Empirical evidence from standardization committees. IEEE Transactions on Engineering Management, 60(1), 148–156.

14 Van de Vrande, V., De Jong, J. P., Vanhaverbeke, W., & De Rochemont, M. (2009). Open innovation in SMEs: Trends, motives and management challenges. Technovation, 29(6–7), 423–437.

15 Mittal, S., Khan, M. A., Romero, D., & Wuest, T. (2018). A critical review of smart manufacturing & Industry 4.0 maturity models: Implications for small and medium-sized enterprises (SMEs). Journal of Manufacturing Systems, 49, 194–214.

16 Gökalp, E., Şener, U., & Eren, P. E. (2017). Development of an assessment model for industry 4.0: Industry 4.0-MM. International Conference on Software Process Improvement and Capability Determination, 128–142.

17 Amershi, S., Begel, A., Bird, C., DeLine, R., Gall, H., Kamar, E., Nagappan, N., Nushi, B., & Zimmermann, T. (2019). Software engineering for machine learning: A case study. 2019 IEEE/ACM 41st International Conference on Software Engineering: Software Engineering in Practice (ICSE-SEIP), 291–300.

18 Wortmann, F., & Flüchter, K. (2015). Internet of things. Business & Information Systems Engineering, 57(3), 221–224.

19 Gilchrist, A. (2016). For IoT reference architecture viewed from different functional perspectives (like technical, operational, business, etc.). see: Industry 4.0: The industrial internet of things. Springer.

20 Bilgeri, D., Gebauer, H., Fleisch, E., & Wortmann, F. (2019). Driving process innovation with IoT field data. MIS Quarterly Executive, 18, 191–207.

21 We broadly discuss the evolutionary stages following: (1) Bilgeri, D., Gebauer, H., Fleisch, E., & Wortmann, F. (2019). Driving process innovation with IoT field data. MIS Quarterly Executive, 18, 191–207, and (2) Herterich, M. M., Uebernickel, F., & Brenner, W. (2016). Stepwise evolution of capabilities for harnessing digital data streams in data-driven industrial services. MIS Quarterly Executive, 15(4).

22 Esmaeilian, B., Sarkis, J., Lewis, K., & Behdad, S. (2020). "Imagine a ledger with encrypted data recorded on it, where different users have access to information based on a set of predefined rules in a smart contract that defines the level and authority of each user in accessing, recording, retrieving, and evaluating data." Blockchain for the future of sustainable supply chain management in Industry 4.0. Resources, Conservation and Recycling, 163, 105064.

23 Catalini, C., & Gans, J. S. (2020). Some simple economics of the blockchain. Communications of the ACM, 63(7), 80–90.

24 Bumblauskas, D., Mann, A., Dugan, B., & Rittmer, J. (2020). A blockchain use case in food distribution: Do you know where your food has been? International Journal of Information Management, 52, 102008.

25 Following Porter, M. E. (1985)., We treat value chain to be the set of activities performed by a given firm, and supply chain to be equivalent to an industry value chain that represents processes involved in producing a particular good or service by one or more firms. Reference: Poter, M. E. (1985). Competitive advantage: Creating and sustaining superior performance. FreePress, New York, NY: FreePress.

26 Lee, H. L., Padmanabhan, V., & Whang, S. (1997). Information distortion in a supply chain: The bullwhip effect. Management Science, 43(4), 546–558.

27 Esmaeilian, B., Sarkis, J., Lewis, K., & Behdad, S. (2020). Blockchain for the future of sustainable supply chain management in Industry 4.0. Resources, Conservation and Recycling, 163, 105064.

28 Wang, H., Chen, K., & Xu, D. (2016). A maturity model for blockchain adoption. Financial Innovation, 2(1), 1–5.
29 Jordan, M. I., & Mitchell, T. M. (2015). Machine learning: Trends, perspectives, and prospects. Science, 349(6245), 255–260.
30 Refer to: Taddy, M. (2019). The technological elements of artificial intelligence. University of Chicago Press, Chicago, IL.
31 Bécue, A., Praça, I., & Gama, J. (2021). Artificial intelligence, cyber-threats and Industry 4.0: Challenges and opportunities. Artificial Intelligence Review, 54(5), 3849–3886.
32 Chen, H., Chiang, R. H., & Storey, V. C. (2012). Business intelligence and analytics: From big data to big impact. MIS Quarterly, 1165–1188.
33 Ghezzi, C., Jazayeri, M., & Mandrioli, D. (1991). Fundamentals of software engineering. Prentice-Hall, Inc.
34 Dennis, A., Wixom, B. H., & Roth, R. M. (2018). Systems analysis and design. John Wiley & Sons.
35 Stoica, M., Mircea, M., & Ghilic-Micu, B. (2013). Software development: Agile vs. Traditional. Informatica Economica, 17(4/2013), 64–76. https://doi.org/10.12948/issn14531305/17.4.2013.06
36 Mell, P., & Grance, T. (2011). The NIST definition of cloud computing.
37 Cito, J., Leitner, P., Fritz, T., & Gall, H. C. (2015). The making of cloud applications: An empirical study on software development for the cloud. Proceedings of the 2015 10th Joint Meeting on Foundations of Software Engineering, 393–403.
38 Senapathi, M., Buchan, J., & Osman, H. (2018). DevOps capabilities, practices, and challenges: Insights from a case study. Proceedings of the 22nd International Conference on Evaluation and Assessment in Software Engineering 2018, 57–67.
39 Leite, L., Rocha, C., Kon, F., Milojicic, D., & Meirelles, P. (2019). A survey of DevOps concepts and challenges. ACM Computing Surveys (CSUR), 52(6), 1–35.
40 Shahin, M., Babar, M. A., & Zhu, L. (2016). The intersection of continuous deployment and architecting process: Practitioners' perspectives. Proceedings of the 10th ACM/IEEE International Symposium on Empirical Software Engineering and Measurement, 1–10.
41 James Lewis, J, & and Martin Fowler, M. (2014). Microservices. Retrieved from: https://www.martinfowler.com/articles/microservices.html
42 Cito, J., Leitner, P., Fritz, T., & Gall, H. C. (2015). The making of cloud applications: An empirical study on software development for the cloud. Proceedings of the 2015 10th Joint Meeting on Foundations of Software Engineering, 393–403.
43 Amershi, S., Begel, A., Bird, C., DeLine, R., Gall, H., Kamar, E., Nagappan, N., Nushi, B., & Zimmermann, T. (2019). Software engineering for machine learning: A case study. 2019 IEEE/ACM 41st International Conference on Software Engineering: Software Engineering in Practice (ICSE-SEIP), 291–300.
44 Sculley, D., Holt, G., Golovin, D., Davydov, E., Phillips, T., Ebner, D., Chaudhary, V., Young, M., Crespo, J.-F., & Dennison, D. (2015). Hidden technical debt in machine learning systems. Advances in Neural Information Processing Systems, 2503–2511.
45 Zaharia, M., Chen, A., Davidson, A., Ghodsi, A., Hong, S. A., Konwinski, A., Murching, S., Nykodym, T., Ogilvie, P., & Parkhe, M. (2018). Accelerating the machine learning lifecycle with MLflow. IEEE Data Engineering Bulletin, 41(4), 39–45.
46 Dennis, A., Wixom, B. H., & Roth, R. M. (2018). Systems analysis and design. John Wiley & Sons.
47 CMU, M. L. D. (2020, August 31). The importance of domain knowledge. Machine learning blog | ML@CMU | Carnegie Mellon University. https://blog.ml.cmu.edu/2020/08/31/1-domain-knowledge/
48 Davenport, T. H., & Patil, D. J. (2012). Data scientist. Harvard Business Review, 90(5), 70–76.

49 Xu, H., Yu, W., Griffith, D., & Golmie, N. (2018). A survey on industrial Internet of Things: A cyber-physical systems perspective. IEEE Access, 6, 78238–78259.

50 See: (1) Hummer, W., Muthusamy, V., Rausch, T., Dube, P., El Maghraoui, K., Murthi, A., & Oum, P. (2019). Modelops: Cloud-based lifecycle management for reliable and trusted AI. 2019 IEEE International Conference on Cloud Engineering (IC2E), 113–120. (2) Amershi, S., Begel, A., Bird, C., DeLine, R., Gall, H., Kamar, E., Nagappan, N., Nushi, B., & Zimmermann, T. (2019). Software engineering for machine learning: A case study. 2019 IEEE/ACM 41st International Conference on Software Engineering: Software Engineering in Practice (ICSE-SEIP), 291–300.

51 Jordan, M. I., & Mitchell, T. M. (2015). Machine learning: Trends, perspectives, and prospects. Science, 349(6245), 255–260.

52 Amershi, S., Begel, A., Bird, C., DeLine, R., Gall, H., Kamar, E., Nagappan, N., Nushi, B., & Zimmermann, T. (2019). Software engineering for machine learning: A case study. 2019 IEEE/ACM 41st International Conference on Software Engineering: Software Engineering in Practice (ICSE-SEIP), 291–300.

53 Sculley, D., Holt, G., Golovin, D., Davydov, E., Phillips, T., Ebner, D., Chaudhary, V., Young, M., Crespo, J.-F., & Dennison, D. (2015). Hidden technical debt in machine learning systems. Advances in Neural Information Processing Systems, 2503–2511.

54 Amershi, S., Begel, A., Bird, C., DeLine, R., Gall, H., Kamar, E., Nagappan, N., Nushi, B., & Zimmermann, T. (2019). Software engineering for machine learning: A case study. 2019 IEEE/ACM 41st International Conference on Software Engineering: Software Engineering in Practice (ICSE-SEIP), 291–300.

55 Amershi, S., Begel, A., Bird, C., DeLine, R., Gall, H., Kamar, E., Nagappan, N., Nushi, B., & Zimmermann, T. (2019). Software engineering for machine learning: A case study. 2019 IEEE/ACM 41st International Conference on Software Engineering: Software Engineering in Practice (ICSE-SEIP), 291–300.

56 Zaharia, M., Chen, A., Davidson, A., Ghodsi, A., Hong, S. A., Konwinski, A., Murching, S., Nykodym, T., Ogilvie, P., & Parkhe, M. (2018). Accelerating the machine learning lifecycle with MLflow. IEEE Data Engineering Bulletin, 41(4), 39–45.

57 Dossani, R., & Kenney, M. (2007). The next wave of globalization: Relocating service provision to India. World Development, 35(5), 772–791.

58 Kamath, R., & Venumuddala, V. (2021). This quote is based on our study and published in one of our published cases. Software and/or Data: Dilemmas in an AI Research Lab of an Indian IT Organization. HBR Store. https://store.hbr.org/product/software-and-or-data-dilemmas-in-an-ai-research-lab-of-an-indian-it-organization/IMB889

59 Kamath, R., & Venumuddala, V. (2021). For a detailed understanding as to why the cloud architect, a senior role within this lab believes this, refer to our case. Software and/or Data: Dilemmas in an AI Research Lab of an Indian IT Organization. HBR Store. https://store.hbr.org/product/software-and-or-data-dilemmas-in-an-ai-research-lab-of-an-indian-it-organization/IMB889

60 Abadi, M., Barham, P., Chen, J., Chen, Z., Davis, A., Dean, J., Devin, M., Ghemawat, S., Irving, G., & Isard, M. (2016). Tensorflow: A system for large-scale machine learning. 12th USENIX Symposium on Operating Systems Design and Implementation OSDI 16, 265–283.

61 NASSCOM. (2018). Talent Demand and Supply Report, AI and Big Data Analytics. National Association of Software and Service Companies.

62 See: Economic Times. (2020, March 16). Covid-19 impact: IT firms seek client waivers so staff can work from home. https://economictimes.indiatimes.com/tech/ites/covid-19-impact-it-firms-seek-client-waivers-so-staff-can-work-from-home/articleshow/74642447.cms; News18. (2020, April 9). Work from home: If the

experiment works, it can continue when the world is better again. https://www.news18.com/news/tech/work-from-home-if-the-experiment-works-it-can-continue-when-the-world-is-better-again-2561401.html

63 TOI. (2020). Microsoft employees can work from home (or anywhere) forever, Times of India. https://www.gadgetsnow.com/tech-news/microsoft-employees-can-work-from-home-or-anywhere-forever/amp_articleshow/78575506.cms

64 Venumuddala, V. R., & Kamath, R. (2022). Work systems in the Indian information technology (IT) industry delivering artificial intelligence (AI) solutions and the challenges of work from home. Information Systems Frontiers, 1–25.

65 Herbsleb, J. D., & Mockus, A. (2003). An empirical study of speed and communication in globally distributed software development. IEEE Transactions on Software Engineering, 29(6), 481–494.

66 Hummer, W., Muthusamy, V., Rausch, T., Dube, P., El Maghraoui, K., Murthi, A., & Oum, P. (2019). Modelops: Cloud-based lifecycle management for reliable and trusted AI. 2019 IEEE International Conference on Cloud Engineering (IC2E), 113–120; Wu, J. (n.d.). ModelOps is the key to enterprise AI. Forbes. Retrieved May 29, 2021, from https://www.forbes.com/sites/cognitiveworld/2020/03/31/modelops-is-the-key-to-enterprise-ai/

4 The Indian IT industry and emerging technologies

Mobility of engineers

In this chapter, we seek to understand the mobility prospects of engineers working in the emerging technology space through our work ethnography in the AI research lab of ITSO. Focusing on the beginner roles working in the emerging technology space – particularly AI and Cloud – we compare the mobility prospects of individuals who come from diverse engineering disciplines. Based on a precursor ethnographic study that we conducted in an Indian engineering college, we connect the disciplinary divide seen in this lab to a similar divide that is manifesting in the engineering education landscape of the country. We end this chapter by discussing the possible role that the Indian IT industry could play in mitigating such a divide, particularly in the context of future emerging technologies. Before going into the discussion based on our ethnographic study, we introduce the role of engineers in the Indian industry in general and IT industry in particular by tracing the coevolutionary dynamic between the Indian industry and the landscape of engineering education in the country.

4.1 Role of engineers in the Indian industry

4.1.1 Engineers and public sector employment

The demands from industry have historically been the key drivers for the evolution of engineering education in India. The early efforts in this evolution occurred in pre-independent British India where engineering jobs were concentrated in military, public works, and railways[1]. The setting up of technical schools by the British government was largely intended to supply trained manpower to the public works departments so as to enable the construction of large-scale infrastructure and irrigation projects. The demand back then was mainly around traditional engineering disciplines such as civil, mechanical, and electrical engineering and these engineers were engaged mainly in construction and maintenance activities. After independence, an urgent need for postwar education development in the country triggered the setting up of Indian Institutes of Technology (IITs) and Regional Engineering Colleges (RECs) as institutes of excellence in technical education across the

DOI: 10.1201/9781003324355-4

country. The Institutes of Technology Act, 1961, governs the functioning of IITs as autonomous entities and links to each other through a common council. Post 2007, the RECs were transformed into National Institutes of Technologies (NITs), governed by the National Institutes of Technology Act, 2007 – placing them on similar lines of operation and autonomy as the IITs. Academic autonomy allowed these institutes to become flexible. This flexibility is important in terms of allowing interdisciplinary coursework to students – and therefore being continuously responsive to the developments in the industry. Besides the IITs and NITs, few autonomous private engineering colleges were on-par with them[2]. Demand from public sector undertakings triggered the demand for several other engineering disciplines, such as chemical, metallurgy, electronics, telecommunications, aeronautical, mining, etc., in addition to the previously existing ones[3]. Until the early 1990s, 85% of the post-matriculate employment was in the public sector. The state was seen as a supplier of engineers from its autonomous IITs and NITs on the one hand and simultaneously generating demands for jobs within public sector industries on the other[4].

4.1.2 Demand from the IT industry and mushrooming of private engineering colleges

A new wave started during the late 1980s and took shape in the 1990s, when growth of Information Technology (IT) in India was accompanied by a mushrooming of privately funded, nonautonomous engineering colleges, to meet the growing demand from the IT industry. During the initial period, the Indian IT services companies sent high-skilled software engineers and programmers to work as consultants for clients in the United States[5]. Tax incentives and setting up exclusive software technology parks in urban metropolitan areas of the country complemented an availability of a large pool of engineering graduates, making this sector slowly shed its image of 'body-shopping' and move up the services value chain[6]. The Indian IT services organizations became characteristically different vis-à-vis the previously dominant employers in the country – manufacturing sector organizations and public sector undertakings. They had flatter hierarchies, promotion, and pay structures were delinked with seniority, and switching employment across organizations within this sector was relatively easier[7]. Having mastered their software service-delivery workflows, these organizations have become leading offshore-service providers for clients across the globe, whose influence brought new cultures of work into these organizations[8]. The standard workflows also allowed these organizations to mitigate the negative effects of work dispersion in a globally distributed software development context that characterized IT offshoring work[9].

As the industry came to be known for providing generic software and business process services to its global clients, it attracted engineering graduates irrespective of their disciplines. Even though engineers from IT-related disciplines like computer science (CS) and IT were better aligned to the work performed in this sector, those from other disciplines were equally in demand. Engineering education was considered to impart a 'set of problem-solving skills, methods of thinking logically and learning tools that help quick adaptation to changes in technology, domains, and tasks'[10]. Disciplinary backgrounds of engineers were therefore less important in comparison to their ability to adapt to changing expectations of work within this industry. Trainings were continually provided by the IT services organizations to mold such engineers into 'generic programmers'[11] who could ramp up to any software platform that a particular client's project was built upon. Preference for engineers also became an important way for the Indian IT services organizations to signal quality to their clients[12]. These organizations have also facilitated appropriate career progression or mobility ladders for such engineers toward project management or other senior technical roles to avoid employee attrition[13].

Engineering slowly became the preferred socially aspiring profession, owing mainly to this IT industry growth. Consequently, a spurt in the number of private engineering colleges was witnessed, because there were a limited number of seats and the entry barriers for admission into IITs and NITs[14] were high. These engineering colleges were funded through the private initiatives of businesses, religious and missionary trusts, charitable organizations, and other non-state actors. Such colleges grew at a disproportionately higher rate in states like Karnataka, Andhra Pradesh, Tamil Nadu, and Maharashtra relative to rest of the country[15]. The distribution of engineering colleges in these regions closely mirrored the distribution of IT services organizations[16]. For most of them, state control was pervasive in terms of enforcing standards around departmental structure, curriculum, and accreditation requirements. They lack the necessary academic autonomy found among the IITs and NITs. These nonautonomous engineering colleges are today a key segment in the Indian engineering education landscape. They graduate close to one million engineers every year – which is roughly equal to 90% of the total engineers graduating from across all institutes in India[17].

4.1.3 Rising demand for emerging technology workforce

The industry is expecting to generate demand for skills around emerging technologies such as AI, Internet of Things (IoT), and Cloud technologies fuelled by digital transformation across industry verticals – the fourth industrial revolution or Industry 4.0[18]. The IT services organizations and the field of engineering education in the country now find themselves at the cusp of another imminent transition. As we saw in the previous chapters, the Indian IT industry is at present, garnering expertise in these new-age technologies, and aspiring to become a leading service provider of digital transformation solutions to its global clients[19]. The calling of Industry 4.0 leads to a different set of expectations from engineers. Engineers from other non-IT engineering disciplines are expected to contribute substantively toward this through their specialized domain knowledge[20]. Such domain knowledge is considered paramount in shaping IT and emerging technology solutions to suit a particular firm and industry context[21]. Therefore, engineers who can handle IT and emerging technologies in addition to contributing with their own discipline-specific expertise could be in great demand for the future requirements of the Indian industry.

Demand for engineers toward the new work roles – for example, data engineers and data scientists within AI, cloud engineers, and cloud architects within Cloud – has been increasing significantly over the past decade. It is becoming evident that this industry which was already in a transition toward emerging technologies is now also poised to benefit immensely owing to the effects of the recent pandemic. Several industry verticals are now demanding solutions around these technologies, realizing their importance for overall operational cost-reduction and sustaining themselves in the post-pandemic era when remote work is expected to increase. To address this demand for work roles of emerging technologies, many established Indian IT services organizations have increased recruitment for these new roles[22]. They are also making efforts to reskill their existing workforce toward these new technologies[23].

In the following section, we look at ITSO's AI research lab through the perspective of some important work roles engaging in the space of AI and Cloud. We lay emphasis on the work of beginner roles so that we could highlight the mobility prospects of engineers from different engineering disciplines in the subsequent sections.

4.2 AI research lab – work roles in an AI project

In the ITSO's AI research lab which we studied, data engineers, and cloud/ software engineers are the beginner roles who primarily worked in the hands-on execution and deployment of AI projects. Cloud architects and junior and senior data scientists are relatively senior work roles and were involved more in devising high-level execution strategies, advising or mentoring beginner roles during the execution of these projects. In addition to the technological requirements underpinning AI projects, such as the aspects related to Machine Learning (ML) and Software Engineering (SW), the beliefs and expectations of the senior managerial and technical work roles also played a crucial role in shaping the work of the beginner roles in this research lab.

The AI project taken up by this lab, in which the ethnographer worked as an intern on an ongoing project along with the data engineers Harish and Vinod, consisted of three main activities. It revolved around natural language processing (NLP), where textual data – in the form of documents or process logs – formed the inputs. Preprocessing input textual data to extract numerical features was the first activity that required data engineers to write programs in platforms such as R or Python. Extracted numerical features give structure to an otherwise unstructured textual data, and allow for experimentation with basic to advanced ML models to provide descriptive, predictive, or prescriptive output. This was the second activity. The third activity involved integrating preprocessing and ML programs, writing wrappers and user interfaces for them, and deploying them over the cloud so that clients could access them remotely and expose their real-time data to these programs. This activity is typically executed by cloud or software (SW) engineers. Automatic extraction of certain kinds of elements[24] from these documents or process logs is the end goal of automation through AI. The output of AI solutions is then manually validated by the Business Process Outsourcing (BPO) workforce engaged in the final data entry so that the resulting combination, AI plus manual work, results in giving very-high accuracy levels (~99% as per Kamal, the business analyst) expected by clients.

4.2.1 Business analysts – developing high-level frameworks

As discussed, the client-centric AI projects taken up by this lab are mainly around augmenting the mainstream IT-BPM services of their clients through the help of AI. Given this scenario, many of the activities that underpin client-service provider interactions in the implementation of the IT-BPM projects of this organization, continued even in the context of the AI projects. One such activity is the regular presentation to the client of high-level frameworks or maps constituting the potential AI solution(s) and what AI use-cases it (they) can solve. In the beginning stages of the current project, the team lead of this lab expected Kamal, the business analyst, to prepare such high-level strategies or frameworks for the purpose of presenting them to clients during client-vendor meetings. These high-level frameworks captured (1) plans to customize or reuse existing IPs for this project and (2) potential costs that the lab could incur in developing and maintaining this project. Based on such frameworks, negotiations around key performance indicators (KPIs) associated with the project, progress of the project, and cost of resources – human or otherwise – incurred during the project are made with the clients.

The high-level frameworks are formulated based on the potential AI augmentation use-cases or requirements that could arise in the client's project. Business analysts usually elicit such requirements directly from clients during the usual client-vendor meetings. They also source for such projects by witnessing the client business process management work first-hand, along with the project managers and data scientists. For the current project, which involved extraction of fields from the client's legal documents (contracts), Kamal carried out both these activities along with the team lead and Sruthi, the data scientist. They had come up with a high-level strategy to customize and reuse some of the existing NLP-related IPs worked out previously by this lab. Sruthi who was also a part of building these IPs knew which ones would be suitable for the client's potential AI use-cases and helped Kamal in refining the high-level strategy/framework. Typically, when clients require the development of new AI implementation strategies, the data scientists build prototype solutions. Sruthi led a related prototype solution that required extraction of a very small sample of should-be-extracted fields (close to 10) from an off-the-shelf collection of documents. Since it was already in its final stages, she had implemented an appropriate strategy for preprocessing the documents and chalked out suitable ML models to learn where in a document one could locate such fields. Her strategy was suitable for the synthetic collection of documents she worked on, and a limited set of fields that she chose for showcasing a working prototype. The current project was similar to this prototype use-case, but it expected a full-fledged AI solution that should be able to extract, with a certain level of accuracy, a very large set of contract elements or fields (such as names, addresses, clauses, and so on) from the real contractual documents that the client wanted to be soon digitalized.

Kamal received a very limited sample of client's old but real contractual documents so that the team could work on 'productionizing' a full-fledged AI solution. In his high-level framework, drawing from Sruthi's work and her inputs, Kamal articulated the preprocessing strategies that the data engineers in this team, Harish and Vinod, could adopt. He also divided the complete set (close to 150) of should-be-extracted contract elements between the two. He wanted the two data engineers to complete the preprocessing work within a stipulated period so that they could connect it with the ML modeling pipeline that Sruthi had already developed for her prototype solution and deploy them together for the client to use.

4.2.2 AI-specific roles – less of use-case-centric productionizing

The data engineers and cloud/software engineers undertake a full-fledged 'productionizing' of any AI solution. Productionizing here refers to scaling up the prototype solutions to cover client's requirements comprehensively and deploying the resulting solutions onto cloud. Since productionizing is the most time-consuming stage of a project, data scientists are formally excluded from this stage, although they informally advise data engineers and oversee the overall project progress. Business analysts and project managers oversee the time and work of data engineers along the high-level frameworks during weekly project status meetings. The team lead also chairs such meetings once a month to assess the progress of the project and the resources it is using up.

In the current project, Harish and Vinod, the data engineers, were made responsible for productionizing the solution along with Sameer and Javed, the cloud/software engineers. They had to follow the high-level framework set by Kamal. Although Sruthi's inputs had gone into building such a framework, her role in the productionizing was limited to informally helping out the data engineers with the challenges they might face. Sruthi was aware that leaving data engineers to follow the high-level framework and work on preprocessing tasks in isolation was not the right strategy, especially given that the client's full-fledged data had a different nature of documents (contractual) and entirely different structure within which the contract elements were embedded.

> *In software [development] it [work to be done] is very clear. Once the high-level design is ready, everyone can start working, and dependence on client is very low. However, in AI, there is data dependency with the client. ML [Machine Learning] Models need to be retrained whenever the nature of data changes.*
>
> (Sruthi, Data Scientist)

She believes that understanding the nature of data pertaining to a particular business use-case is central to AI projects. The reading of data in domain like logistics will be very different from a reading of data from say, the financial sector or health care. Unlike traditional software development, which revolves around software programs and modules, ML or AI projects are centered around a particular use-case and its corresponding data[25]. Despite its importance, clients are seldom open to sharing their full data, citing security concerns. In the initial stages of any project, clients share only a very preliminary set of data that lacks the volume and variety required to experiment with different ML models. The current project is a good example of this where only 30 older contractual documents were shared by the clients for the data engineers to work on a full-fledged solution. On top of this, clients are reluctant to accept solutions that are not easily explainable. Since clients want solutions that can be explained simply and clearly, advanced deep learning models whose outputs are relatively inexplicable are typically excluded while working on client-centric AI projects.

It is only after deployment that the clients share the full real-time data through secure interfaces. Therefore, till deployment, data engineers work mainly on preprocessing the available client data to extract important features. For example, in this project, Harish and Vinod were building on the preprocessing codes written by Sruthi for her previous project where she built prototype solution for a similar NLP project. During weekly project status meetings, the business analyst and project manager evaluate the data engineers' work on metrics around customization, reuse, and clear division of tasks. The ethnographer attended these meetings along with Kamal, the business analyst, and the data engineers, Harish and Vinod. The team lead believed that this is important because it saves costs as one does not have to work things out from scratch. As discussed before, in this project, the preprocessing tasks were divided and allocated between Harish and Vinod, and both were asked to customize and reuse existing work done by Sruthi in her previous project where she built the prototype. Often Kamal also used to step in the shoes of a project manager and expect a relatively clear task division between data engineers (who would be working on more than one project at a time) to account for the cost of human resources taken up in the current project. Sruthi believes that this way of working is incompatible with the ideal-typical execution of AI projects where the solutions are always use-case centered and require iterative experimentation between team members. This often does not allow for a clear division of tasks or activities. She called the current way of executing projects as inefficient because some use-cases might require working on the two activities, preprocessing and ML model building, simultaneously and iteratively to arrive at a solution.

> *In data-science projects it is important to understand [ML] models from the data [and use case] point of view, and not the program or code point of view … unlike software here the way [of work] is entirely different and needs to be identified based on the nature of data and possible behavior of various ML models … it [work strategy] also has to be dynamically analyzed at every phase as the client data matures with volume and variety during productionizing.*
>
> (Sruthi, Data Scientist)

She also believes that the high-level frameworks guiding the work allocation between software engineers in typical software projects are an inefficient strategy to adopt for AI projects. Software development can be thought of as an integrated whole made up of modular, customizable, and reusable components[26]; as a result, allocating tasks in isolation is a desired strategy. In contrast, to build a use-case optimal AI solution, Sruthi believes that work allocation strategies in the context of AI projects must always keep in mind the use-case and the corresponding data.

4.2.3 Software roles – integration and deployment

One can notice the similarity between Kamal's work in the context of devising high-level frameworks for executing AI projects and Yuvraj, the cloud architect's work, in the context of devising detailed and high-level plans for deploying the resulting solution onto cloud. In the current project, as per such high-level plans that Yuvraj had prescribed, Sameer and Javed, the cloud engineers, were integrating the preprocessing programs developed by the data engineers Harish and Vinod, and ML models that Sruthi had developed previously for her prototype. The high-level plans prepared by cloud architects incorporate the estimated time and computing resources expected by the models or preprocessing programs. Such estimates are critical to plan the usage of cloud resources and associated their associated costs during deployment.

> *[when] clients ask for faster pre-processing [for example], then the cloud architect [should be in a position] to configure or adjust the intermediate architecture in such a way that the resulting micro-service that will be used from the cloud will run faster and reduce the pre-processing time within the overall pipeline of tasks.*
>
> (Yuvraj, Cloud Architect)

According to Yuvraj, it is very critical that the AI modules developed by data engineers or data scientists should be optimized for such time and resource constraints. But given the way preprocessing work is performed across projects in this lab, he doesn't seem to be satisfied with the work of the data engineers, particularly those from non-IT backgrounds, who have less expertise in computer programming.

> *None of the engineers [data-engineers] working on AI solutions are programming as per any high-level architecture framework. This is unlike software projects, where upstream technical blueprints serve as a reference for downstream software engineers. Here I have to wait forever for things to settle down downstream and then ask the cloud engineers to wrap the pre-processing programs into some usable modules or micro-services. We cannot blame the data engineers. They come with little or no programming practice and are recruited mainly from data science or operations management backgrounds. Most of their codes are unorganized and turn out to be terribly slow, and waste so much computing resources when deployed over the Cloud. They do not account for parallelization that is possible in today's computing systems. These data engineers are required to multi-team or work for several projects at a time and don't get enough time to improve their programming skills ... I see no way how we can improve this situation as of now.*

(Yuvraj, Cloud Architect)

Nonetheless, a first-cut solution comprising preprocessing programs and ML models, as discussed above, is wrapped with secure user interfaces and deployed onto the cloud for clients to expose their full volume and variety of data in real time. For this project, the deployment was in cloud, but for many of the previous projects, such a deployment also happened in client's on-premise servers. Nevertheless, the strategy of deployment was largely similar.

4.2.4 Data scientists – building compatible workflows

It was not surprising to find data scientists in this lab complaining about the dominance of software engineering principles and practices which guided the workflows even in AI projects. This dominance goes beyond some of the aspects we discussed such as – (a) customization and reuse of previous project work, (b) attempts at clear task division, and (c) preponderance of activities around high-level frameworks prepared by the business analyst. Sruthi mentions that, even during the prototype development stage, *clients expect week-by-week incremental status updates [following] under agile [sprints] to obtain information about progress of the prototype solution and that too largely in non-technical terms.* It should be mentioned that this is a key stage for data scientists to gain domain knowledge around client use-cases and decide the features to extract from data for preprocessing. Given that the preliminary data shared by the client is rarely sufficient, it also helps in honing down the ML model and the choice of close-enough off-the-shelf data to conduct experimentation. However, Sruthi bemoans that the way work progresses during such proto-type stages, this rarely happens. They have to juggle to make workarounds to keep the client engaged during the agile sprints. In one of the projects, she took the help of the software team to design a UI that displayed in the form of a dashboard, the summary statistics associated with different features or vari-ables extracted from the preliminary client data. In every weekly sprint, she, along with this team, presented the summary statistics and, parallelly, show-cased the analytics strategies that they planned to adopt given these features. She said that *first [dashboard] was to keep them engaged … the second [presentation of analytics strategies] was more technical and innovative.* The dashboard is to help clients differentiate between inputs about features that are important and those that are not so important. Eventually, she says, *how they drill down the UI … will give us indirect cues and feedback for us to build models.* The same holds true during the productionizing stage, when junior data scientists, data engi-neers, cloud/software engineers, and the client teams go through agile sprints to correct issues that pop up when the solution gets deployed in the cloud or on-premise client servers. Following is a paraphrased quote from a conversa-tion with Krishna, the data scientist about his stint as a data engineer in one of his previous projects.

> *Standard SW practices can be a hurdle in ML work. In [agile] sprints, front-end software development and ML model development were clubbed. Our software engineers created an interface for clients … with this interface they could pull dummy data, and show how these things are working … but instead they said, since some model is already there, [so] we will get real data and process. The prob-lem was we have to be in same space like them. They just have to create interface, but we have to create an entire model.*
>
> (Krishna, Data Scientist)

Data scientists of the team are aware of the pitfalls that come with this sway of software engineering practices. They are involved in working toward building workflows that are relatively more compatible with their AI projects. We witnessed one such proposal which was presented by them to some members of the client teams. According to them, ML-specific workflows can provide platforms that could facilitate iterative experi-mentation between work roles engaged in the interrelated and use-case driven work activities – preprocessing and model building – in AI projects. Such workflows are expected to promote greater use-case and data-centric collaboration than the current way of working. They believe that this will allow the lab not only to achieve better accuracies from their AI solutions but also to scale such solutions to multiple clients. Such workflows require appropriate integration of version-control-based software programs that are better known to programmers. Two data scientists having this pro-gramming expertise, in addition theoretical knowledge of statistics and

ML, have taken this responsibility in the team. The team lead, Krishna, and Sruthi are overseeing this effort, and they expect to deploy these new workflows in the near future.

4.3 Mobility prospects of beginner roles

4.3.1 Data engineers and their mobility pathways

From the discussion above, it is clear that data engineers were predominantly allocated the activity of preprocessing the data, and data scientists were involved in building ML models. The reason for this was to do, primarily with the ease of dividing preprocessing tasks among multiple data engineers. In the current project, where preprocessing of data required extracting fields from text documents, Kamal, the business analyst divided the fields between the two data engineers, Harish and Vinod, assigned for this project. This preprocessing activity was largely about writing rule-based software programs to extract such fields. Here, data engineers with different levels of programming expertise had their own strategies for writing programs. Among the two, Vinod was an experienced software programmer and Harish had an industrial engineering background and was recruited by this team for his understanding of operations management and data sciences. While working with these two in the project, the ethnographer observed that Vinod, who was an expert programmer, identified programs by their abstractions, modularity, interfacing requirements, and other features characteristic of object-oriented design within software development. Harish, on the other hand, who had only a working knowledge of programming relied entirely on online forums while writing programs. The following observation by the ethnographer brings out the difference between expertise and working knowledge of programming.

> *Those having expertise in Computer Programming look at programs through a set of constructs, which lets them imagine what each line of code is doing in a much richer manner, in comparison to those not having formal training or practice in computer programming. For some, understanding of the program is limited by the kind of codes they have to write for Data Analytics. Coding communities, especially those working on open-source programming languages like python, are making efforts to make the functions within packages as abstract as possible, so that just with a click of a button one can give requisite inputs and get the desired output. However, in many instances, data-engineers encounter problems where one has to debug codes written by others. In such cases, those lacking programming expertise prefer to have experts debug and correct the code, instead of them trying out on their own.*

(Observations, Field notes)

With the pressure of project deadlines and such a motley mix of experts and non-experts writing programs, it was difficult for the lab to build an efficient solution stack, suitable for eventual customization and reuse. Team members often exchanged their work in an ad-hoc manner.

4.3.1.1 Data sciences and business understanding

For the senior data scientists, many of whom were PhDs, knowledge about the theoretical underpinnings of various ML models was more important than having expertise in programming. Since most of their work relied on off-the-shelf data to build IPs for the team, for them, working knowledge of programming sufficed. During the project, these data scientists pushed data engineers to understand (1) what kind of features are relevant in the data for the client's use-case and (2) what ML models are plausible given such features. While the former requires data engineers to have a business understanding of the client's project, the latter requires them to have theoretical training in data sciences. However, with the pressure of deadlines from the business analysts and project managers, these data engineers spent most of their time building rule-based preprocessing programs. This resulting separation of technical and client-facing activities made use-case-centric experimentation of AI solution development difficult. This was clear from the way the current project was being productionized.

Most data engineers in this team had backgrounds in industrial engineering (a non-IT discipline), but since their work dealt more with traditional software programming, they failed to transpose their prior engineering skills onto such work.

> We want to eventually end up in a data science position, since the concepts associated with it are close to what we learnt in college, such as courses like statistics, optimization, and other subjects related to operations and supply chains.
>
> (Harish, Data-engineer from an industrial engineering background)

Non-IT engineers aspiring to become data scientists were keen to grasp the theoretical underpinnings of ML strategies. Harish was a good example. With his background in industrial engineering and strong foundations in operations and statistics, he was aspiring toward technical or managerial roles such as data scientist, business analyst, or a project manager – engaging substantively with the business understanding of client use-cases. Many such use-cases required client-facing roles to understand firm's value chain activities, or supply chains in general during the requirements elicitation, and even in subsequent stages. Harish felt that such roles were better suited to his Industrial Engineering background.

4.3.1.2 Primacy of programming skills

Most non-IT data engineers like Harish, aspiring for client-facing roles like that of a business analyst or project manager, understood the importance of having a business understanding of the client's use-cases. However, they were struggling and lagging behind their programmer colleagues in similar roles.

> *Sometimes [the] inability in judging the time that will take to code can give the impression to the managers that they are shirking. Their struggle is palpable. They are burning their brains to write programs relying on web sources, and sinking themselves into their computers, rarely moving away from it, trying to learn something or the other, and so on ... The higher-ups, the business analysts and managers, think only in terms of available frameworks and try to divide the tasks, and they often fail to listen to these nuances of the micro-level work, and expect these engineers to figure them out. Clearly, those with SW background having programming expertise and an understanding of processes associated with software development, are better off here.*
>
> (Observation, Field notes)

The above reflection based on the ethnographer's observation during a project status meeting, highlights this issue of IT vs non-IT divide, clearly visible in the context of AI projects in this lab. During this meeting, Harish, the data engineer with an industrial engineering background and having limited programming experience struggled to specify the time he would take to program.

> *Cleaning, organizing, structuring data is a major chunk of work that is given to the data-engineers. This low-end work can be done more efficiently by computer engineers who are adept at programming. Once structured data sets become available, the analysis of data can be done by them [the data engineers having limited programming practice], but these tasks are taken over by the data-scientists.*
>
> (Observation, Field notes)

Given that data engineers have to do programming-based tasks, it was obvious that those having prior programming expertise had an edge. In this lab, the two data scientists who were given the task of building AI-compatible workflows were previously data engineers, expert in software programming. Both of them had worked as software developers before doing their Masters in data sciences and industrial engineering streams. Trained software engineers thus seemed to be more suited for the data scientist positions, provided they could complement their programming knowledge with additional data-science courses. One of the junior data scientists echoed this, *many software developers are applying [to data science positions] ... they do some data analytics projects, take some [online certification] courses.* Another example is one of the software architects from an adjacent team who successfully transitioned from a software role to a data science-related role. She says,

> *I have done my B. Tech in computer science and worked for close to 10 years until now.... I am now taking lot of data-science courses, mainly by clearing online*

certification courses that are being offered … goal is to end up in AI/ML related work-role sometime in the future.… The main reason for this is also because having worked for so many years in this industry I have worked more or less in all possible technical roles … I don't have interest in taking up managerial roles in this industry.… But AI/ML offers newer technical roles and is now in high-demand … I would like to take up a role that is at the intersection of software and data-sciences.

From the observations and aspirations expressed during work, it was evident that data engineers having no prior software programming expertise struggle to access their aspirational positions – technical data scientists or managerial roles. Given the kind of environment they work in, their lack of programming expertise waylays their aspirations. Coping up with programming-related tasks takes up most of their time.

4.3.2 Cloud/software engineers and their mobility pathways

Compute Engines reside in the cloud, maintained by the cloud service providers. Whatever AI models we develop, that will need some APIs [Application Programming Interfaces] which need to sit in the web-server so that inputs are taken, pre-processed, models run, and outputs post-processed using the compute engines in the cloud. API creation will need dedicated software engineers who are experts at cloud. Cloud engineers [therefore] are very crucial in deploying the AI algorithms into cloud or on-premise servers.

(Sameer, Cloud Engineer)

Cloud/software engineers are responsible for stitching preprocessing and ML programs, building wrappers and user interfaces so that clients can access them online. The ethnographer's interaction with these engineers revealed that these engineers are engaged solely in software programming related to solution deployment over cloud.

4.3.2.1 Client-independent standard work requirements

Unlike data engineers who need a sound understanding of the client's business use-cases if they aspire to be future data scientists or business analysts, for cloud/software engineers, a technical understanding of the software is sufficient to carry out their work. These cloud engineers work in the direction set out by cloud architects which are again situated within the cloud/software technical domain. Within this team, cloud architects work at the interstices between AI programs developed by the team and compute resources available on the cloud. The cloud architect defines an intermediate architecture for efficiently managing the allotment of computational resources for different AI programs. Being a senior technical role, the cloud architect is an aspirational role for these engineers. In addition, cloud engineers also opine that the technological advancements in cloud technology are providing cloud or software engineers ample prospects for their future, which are on-par or even better than data scientists. In this regard Sameer says,

> *The AI/ML craze is high because it's often in the news and many companies by deploying these solutions advertise too much. But, even in traditional SW so many developments are happening, like Node.js, Kubernetes and so on, related to cloud. If we include in our resumes that we know these new technologies in Software, our resumes too will attract many recruiters, and not just Data Analysts or scientists.*

For cloud/software engineers, their backgrounds seemed to matter less in their mobility journey. Given the nature of work in the Indian IT sector, many engineers, irrespective of their disciplinary backgrounds, can aspire toward becoming expert programmers by taking up the formal mobility pathway in traditional software or the more recent cloud. Even those from non-IT disciplines have clear means to train themselves within this organization and chart the cloud-related mobility pathway similar to those coming from an IT discipline. The following quote from Javed, a cloud engineer having no prior background in any of the IT engineering disciplines drives this point.

> *I prefer to stick to whatever I am doing now, because it's hard to change after choosing a certain path. I was initially fearful about programming while in college, but after coming here, since I was clear what I had to do here, I picked it up fast and now that fear is gone, I enjoy coding and want to go work in similar kind of stuff in the future.*
>
> (Javed, Cloud Engineer with an Electronics Engineering background)

4.3.3 Mobility challenges of non–IT engineers – the IT and non–IT divide

From the foregoing discussion, it is clear that workflows negotiated between client and ITSO largely govern the AI project work undertaken by the beginner roles in this lab. Such workflows are guided predominantly by software engineering principles as reflected (a) by the expectations of client-facing senior managerial roles – the team lead, business analyst, and project manager and (b) by the observed nature of how the project-related activities were executed in past projects. The expectations of senior managerial roles are driven by the necessity to generate revenue, a priority for this lab to avoid becoming cost center. Their expectations created an artificial, but a clear division of tasks between (i) client-facing activities (like coming up with high-level frameworks) and implementation-related activities, (ii) AI pre-processing activities and ML model-building activities, and (iii) AI-specific activities and the deployment activity. Data engineers, the beginner roles in such projects, were the ones who were caught in this divide.

AI projects run optimally when the use-case and its associated domain structure drives data preprocessing and model-building activities[27]. Here we observe that such activities are allocated to data engineers and data scientists who worked in isolation. Division of work between data engineers was driven by the high-level frameworks devised by the business analyst, and similarly for the cloud engineers it was driven by the strategies devised by the cloud architect. Use-case-centric development was possible only post the solution deployment when full data of client got fed into their AI programs through secure user interfaces developed by cloud engineers. But even during these stages, data engineers were expected to work largely on preprocessing activities under the instructions of data scientists who oversaw model enhancement activities.

Data in AI projects is linked to the client's specific domain and business that requires some domain knowledge. Making an appropriate choice of ML models requires, on the other hand, a theoretical understanding of statistics or ML. The data engineers believed that with their industrial (or other domain-specific) engineering backgrounds, with some efforts, they could easily acquire such theoretical knowledge and business understanding. However, their efforts were hampered by the onerous chore of programming-related tasks that they were assigned to. This was an unintended consequence of the importance given by senior managers to customization, reuse, and clear task allocation, over iterative experimentation between work activities and corresponding roles, even in AI-centric projects. Cost concerns, showcasing incremental status updates to clients, and incompatible project workflows were the key factors leading to this preponderance of software engineering practices in these AI-augmented projects. This, however, did not alter the work environment for cloud and software engineers. Their mobility was driven by the expertise they gained in technical aspects related to software development in the era of cloud, and less around statistical knowledge or business understanding. Irrespective of their prior engineering backgrounds, we observe that they showed motivation to prepare or train themselves to work with software engineering practices.

There was another aspect of AI projects where the data engineers, particularly those from non-IT backgrounds, were found to be at a disadvantage. This was related to the task of building AI-compatible workflows that could facilitate use-case-centered experimentation between different work activities – preprocessing, model building, and deployment. We noticed that as these workflow enhancements required programming expertise in addition to a theoretical understanding of statistics and ML, only those data scientists who had programming backgrounds were chosen. This shows the importance of programming knowledge – on top of statistics or domain knowledge – for data engineers to move up their career ladder. For data engineers from non-IT backgrounds, who were otherwise well situated to grasp the use-case-specific domain knowledge of the client, this is clearly disadvantageous. Their aspirational roles – data scientist and business analyst – required them to transpose and enrich the learnings from their prior educational and occupational backgrounds. However, with the need to stay on par with their colleagues from IT backgrounds, these aspirations were ambushed by the sheer time they were required to spend gaining programming expertise.

When the pandemic necessitated Work from Home (WFH) mandates, there were signs of a further deterioration in the mobility prospects of engineers working in the emerging technology space. In the initial stages of the pandemic, when clients from key sectors closed down their operations, many established Indian IT services organizations sought waivers from the government for 'furloughs and temporary lay-offs of surplus employees'[28]. The buzz was that these organizations might cut down their focus on emerging technology projects, in particular around AI. Advanced data analytics using AI seemed unimportant as the data gathered by clients until now could become obsolete for making meaningful predictions in a very uncertain future[29]. Consequently, concerns were expressed that clients may withhold their advanced AI-based digital transformation projects and fall back on basic descriptive analytics-related projects like before. Such opinions exacerbated the concerns of the engineers working in the emerging technology space as they appeared to be the first ones to get laid-off from such organizations during this period[30].

Fortunately, the situation seemed to have improved soon, and the Indian IT industry thrived despite continued WFH requirements. The Indian government announced a slew of measures to reduce compliance burdens on the IT services companies. Contrary to the opinions floating around in the initial stages of the pandemic-induced closure, clients seemed to lay even a greater emphasis on emerging technologies than before. Based on such trends, many experts now believe that for the Indian IT industry this pandemic could be another Y2K, an event responsible for putting Indian IT on a global pedestal[31]. Many IT service companies have ramped up their recruitment drives significantly for their emerging technology teams, and also announced bonuses and salary hikes for their employees to retain such talent[32]. Although the situation looks promising in general, our findings indicate that a continued WFH in the absence of emerging technology-compatible workflows could only worsen the existing mobility challenges of these engineers. Especially so, for the non-IT engineers in beginner roles who may want to engage their domain-specific expertise relevant to client's business context. Our study shows that the extant workflows, more suitable for distributed software development, could deprive them of such a context leaving them solely at the mercy of their software programming skills.

In addition, the WFH brought added complications in gaining expertise around AI-related projects for the data engineers. The ethnographer noticed that the two data engineers, Harish and Vinod, who used to work in tandem while preparing their status presentations in the office, could not do so when the meetings shifted online. Each of them independently prepared detailed deck of slides indicating his share of work done in the project. In the office, during the status meetings with the business analysts and managers, the two of them often wrote on the board intermittently while presenting their progress of work on the project. Sometimes when their presentations weren't ready, they used to present their status on the board, extempore. However, with WFH, the ethnographer noticed that in every weekly and monthly status meeting, they came with detailed points describing what they had done over that particular week or month and what will they do in the future. They are seen to adhere more to the modular, customization/reuse framework set by the business analyst. They religiously attempted to align their presentations around tasks performed along the expectations set by such a framework. The two data engineers during their presentations in the office were often seen to complement each other while presenting their work; now during the online meetings, one was silent while the other was presenting. The environment in ITSO's research lab allowed the data engineers to gain knowledge about the context of their project and about other projects and also about other kinds of work beyond AI, from their teammates. The ethnographer was part of many such informal discussions that these data engineers had with their lunch mates who were also their college friends. Conversations between them always started with a common question, 'what are you currently working on?' Unknowingly in these conversations, a good amount of talk about the organization, the projects they are working on, and the projects others were working on got passed around. For these data engineers, in the absence of structured workflows, these informal channels were crucial to their gaining that domain-specific knowledge around their projects, which got disrupted by WFH.

4.4 IT vs non-IT divide – manifesting in the engineering colleges

The foregoing discussion highlighted the IT vs non-IT divide around mobility challenges faced by non-IT engineers in the context of moving up the AI ladder at ITSO. In this section, we show that the genesis of this divide stems from the Indian engineering education system supplying these engineers – the so-called foot soldiers for IT services industry in India[33]. Here, we rely on an ethnographic study that we conducted in a nonautonomous private engineering college situated near Bengaluru – which was in fact a precursor to our main ethnographic study at ITSO's research lab. In addition to the two-member research team associated with the ethnography at ITSO, this study was carried out in collaboration with another PhD student[34]. He/she had close contacts with the faculty of this college, which helped us gain access to this college. With support from the college faculty and formal permission from the principal of this college, the ethnographer undertook weekly tutorials in ML and data analytics for third-year electronics students. We clarified our research objective to students and the faculty: which was to understand the mobility prospects of engineering students. The ethnographer, having formal training in statistics and other related subjects during doctoral coursework, was able to design a curriculum to conduct such tutorials. The absence of any formal courses on AI/ML in this college also motivated the faculty to support the ethnographer in this endeavor. During the duration of a semester, the ethnographer visited the college every week, while the PhD student collaborator visited occasionally to help the ethnographer connect with some faculty whom he knew. The ethnographer took a one-hour tutorial every Thursday and during the rest of the time got the opportunity to informally discuss with students, faculty members, and other stakeholders in this college. The ethnographer witnessed placement drives, discussed programming-related projects voluntarily or otherwise undertaken by students from non–IT engineering streams, and understood the career aspirations of students from different non–IT engineering streams across their yearly cohorts. Short memory markers that the ethnographer captured during the day enabled compilation of our ethnographic field notes which were shared and discussed weekly with this three-member research team. While the ethnographer was engrossed in the 'emic' during the fieldwork, our weekly discussion on the field notes included all three researchers, enabling us to get the 'etic' perspective. It helped us to contextualize our findings within the broader engineering education field of the country and accordingly pay attention to relevant objects of inquiry during our subsequent field visits. Our field notes pertaining to ethnography in this engineering college ran into over 40 single-spaced pages in Microsoft Word, amounting to about 40,000 words. Table 4.1 gives overview of major components of our data excluding day-to-day observations.

In relation to the broader context of this chapter, we mainly discuss the influence of IT services industry on this Engineering College and cover the challenges facing non–IT engineers in their emerging technology-related pursuits.

4.4.1 Lack of academic autonomy and rigid disciplinary boundaries

Among the engineering colleges that have grown in parallel to the growth of IT services industry in India, the majority labeled 'nonautonomous' as we saw above, have little autonomy in curriculum-setting and conducting of exams. They are pegged to a Central/State University. Such nonautonomous engineering colleges form the majority in the landscape of Indian engineering education, graduating a staggering 90% of engineers every year across different disciplines[35]. The college that we studied also falls in this category of nonautonomous engineering colleges. It is affiliated to the technical university of Karnataka state. The lack of academic autonomy of an

Table 4.1 Data components

Weekly tutorials

There were in total five modules: 1: Basic Probability and Statistics, 2: Overview of Machine Learning, 3: Supervised Learning Models, 4: Unsupervised Learning, and 5: Social Network Analysis.

Regular interaction with stakeholders beyond tutorial sessions

We visited this college for close to 16 weeks between June–Nov, 2019. Beyond regular impromptu conversations, we also were able to carry out unstructured interviews (UI) of – (1) student groups on different occasions, mostly before/after placement drives and tutorial sessions, (2) faculty from various departments, and (3) HR personnel. These UIs spanned between 30 minutes (with some of the faculty) to over 2 hours (with alumni students). On average most of them were around the 45-minute duration. Following are some details about stakeholders we regularly interacted during fieldwork.

Stakeholders	Details
Faculty	3 from Electronics, 2 from CS, 1 from Mechanical
HR Personnel	1 HR Manager, 5 staff
Students (Electronics Engineering)	8 from 1st year, 24 from 3rd year, 8 from 4th year, 2 Alumni
Students (Computer Science Engineering)	4 from 3rd year
Students (Mechanical Engineering)	4 from 3rd year
Students (Aerospace Engineering)	4 from 1st year
Students (Civil Engineering)	Two 3rd and two 4th year students

affiliated college is clearly articulated as per the National Accreditation Body as follows[36],

> *[an] affiliated College is essentially a teaching unit which depends on a larger body namely university for legitimizing its academic and administrative processes. Its engagement with curricular aspects is mainly in their implementation … [They] have rather insignificant role in curriculum designing and development.*

The college conducts 4-year undergraduate degree programs in engineering disciplines such as CS, Electronics, Mechanical, Civil, and Aerospace. The disciplinary boundaries in this college are rather rigid owing to the lack of academic autonomy. Necessary mechanisms to ensure flexibility for students to pursue interdisciplinary coursework are absent. Autonomous engineering colleges (the Indian Institutes of Technology or IITs, for example), on the other hand, have mechanisms such as offering elective courses to students from across disciplines so that they could equip themselves appropriately for the industry needs. This college, however, has to follow a specific curriculum for each discipline as stipulated by the state university. The state university also evaluates students' performance through external examinations that are commonly held for students from all its affiliated colleges each semester. The faculty and students in this college are therefore strongly attached to their respective disciplines, owing to these formal requirements set by the state university.

4.4.2 A dominant influence of IT industry for student placements

Student placements constitute an important marker in improving the rankings of this college, and the IT Industry of Bengaluru is one of their major recruiters. To facilitate recruiters from the IT industry in conducting on-campus placement drives year-on-year, this college has instituted a separate Human Resources (HR) department and established formal communication channels with prominent IT recruiters from Bengaluru. This department also organizes programming workshops, soft-skills, and communication-skills training to students from across disciplines. In particular, the college alumni, who are now working as software engineers in reputed IT companies, are brought to organize programming workshops. The soft-skills and communication-skills trainers are the same set of people who conduct campus-to-corporate programs in the IT companies situated in Bengaluru. These activities conducted by the HR department of this college are mandatory for all students from their second year onward.

> *Earlier if academically strong, the college was good. Once the IT jobs came … if you are strong in placing students there … your college is good. From marks in university exams, it has now shifted to IT placements.*
>
> (Previous placement-in-charge of this college)

In fact, as per the previous placement-in-charge, this model where a separate HR department drives activities around IT placements is borrowed from a top-ranking private engineering college in Bengaluru. The latter had spearheaded similar activities more than a decade ago and formally created facilities for IT recruiters to conduct large-scale placement drives on their campus. He says that such activities are founded on the belief that the skills they impart to students will be rewarded in the IT industry as the employees are expected to work in cross-cultural environments spread across the globe.

The placement statistics of past 5 years displayed on the college's website are concrete evidence of the disproportionate skew toward placement in the IT sector. In the academic year 2018–2019, in the Mechanical Engineering Department, 19 out of 22 placed students ended up with IT jobs. These numbers were 45 out of 49, and 13 out of 17 respectively for Electronics and Civil Engineering Departments. Similarly, in the first half of academic year 2019–2020, out of 149 placed students from across departments, all of them ended up in IT jobs offered by four major IT giants of Bengaluru. Such statistics are displayed, advertised, and published so that their ranking among other engineering colleges in the state is revealed to the potential students and their guardians. Students also base their decision of joining a particular department or college during their counseling process[37] based on how well a college or a particular discipline (like for example CS vs Mechanical) is ranked with respect to such placements. Placements, particularly in the Indian IT industry, have therefore become an unavoidable reality for these nonautonomous engineering colleges.

4.4.3 Students from non-IT disciplines and their negotiated flexibility toward IT

Although the HR department of this college provided formal avenues for students from non-IT disciplines to get placed into the IT industry, it found difficult to get them placed in their relevant non-IT industries. The HR manager expresses that it is not easy building formal communication channels around placements with industries other than IT. He says, *it is difficult to organize on-campus placements for other departments like electrical, civil or mechanical like we do for IT … IT companies can recruit students from any department … they provide trainings … can maintain reserve pools through their bench policies … all this is not possible for other industries.*

A lack of placements in industries aligned with their own 'core' (students' reference to their own non-IT engineering discipline) is causing disillusionment among many students. Despite the HR training, these students feel disadvantaged when compared to the CS discipline, because their usual coursework fails to prepare them sufficiently with skills around software engineering or programming. For example, one of the mechanical students said, *I attended many IT placement drives, in one went until interview … but didn't get placed because it's all about programming … we don't get to practice programming, [because we are taught] only C language in our 1st year and that too basics, after that we don't have any course [related to programming or software engineering].* Another student from civil engineering similarly expressed his inability to clear IT interviews because of lack of programming practice, *I applied [to an IT company] … went for 3rd round, HR round completed, but they are not satisfied, because we don't know any programming language properly.* The quote by one of the electronics students neatly summarizes this plight of students from non-IT disciplines. Expressing his disillusionment, he says, *if the college knows that everyone at the end will be pushed into IT, why doesn't it give trainings around SQL [software database related language] or Java programming to all the department students like they give soft-skills trainings … across all four years of our study.*

Notwithstanding this, the non-IT students and the faculty have negotiated a peculiar flexibility toward ensuring their fit toward IT placements. Students from such disciplines take up, what are called, 'mini-projects' that involve working on their own discipline-specific problem but also requiring them to work on programming-related aspects. According to students, these projects serve as important talking point during the IT interviews. Students take up such projects either voluntarily or with support from the faculty. In particular, when some students find it difficult to take up such projects voluntarily, the faculty consciously supports them by grouping them with others who are good at programming. They further substitute such mini-projects for the regular coursework-related assignments[38]. Since there is a rigidity around their own discipline-specific curriculum, faculty attempt to increase the time spent by students on those subjects in their curriculum which are relatively better recognized by the IT recruiters. For example, in one instance, the head of electronics department directed the faculty responsible for 'signal processing and networks' course, to allocate more lab-time for this subject. She said that this subject within electronics seems to be attractive to the recruiters from IT as informed to her by the principal of this college.

4.4.4 Students from non-IT disciplines and emerging technology pursuits

We observed that many students from non-IT disciplines recognize that the next big things in the industry are emerging technology roles and they need to prepare themselves in this regard. Some of them took up mini-projects that are at the intersection of their respective disciplines, IT, and emerging technologies (AI in particular). Students were discussing ideas like 'developing automated health tracking systems for livestock', 'automated systems to pre-empt heavy power disruptions that are currently prevalent in rural areas', etc. Since their curriculum didn't offer any courses in this space, they were relying on online courses and sought short-term training and unpaid internships to build their skills in these areas. Numerous posters of private training agencies offering such training with some promising unpaid internships were pasted on the college noticeboards for students to see and apply.

Despite the students' interests around emerging technologies, such interests seem to get waylaid in the college's disproportionate emphasis on IT placements. For instance, a recent initiative by the government to establish entrepreneurial tinkering labs in some of these colleges provided an avenue for students from non-IT disciplines to work on their discipline-related problems and lays special emphasis on employing emerging technologies like AI and IoT. However, we noticed that many of the students who participated in this initiative from the college wanted to engage in these projects only because such projects would help in enriching their resumes in the context of cracking IT job interviews during on-campus placement drives.

4.5 Scope for substantive engagement of non-IT engineers in the IT industry

Our findings from ITSO's research lab indicated that engineers from non-IT disciplines, occupying beginner roles in the space of AI, face a big challenge in their career progression to senior roles in the emerging technology space – like that of the data scientist. Their training makes them better positioned to engage in roles that require a substantive understanding of client's use-case, falling within a particular industry or a firm's business domain. But a predominance of software engineering work assigned to these engineers, despite their limited exposure, is a bottleneck. The foregoing discussion also highlighted the struggles of non-IT engineers of an engineering college in the context of building skills at the intersection of emerging technologies and their core disciplines – a combination that is expected to be vital for industries in the context of industry 4.0. In essence, the IT vs non-IT divide that is visible in the context of IT services organizations has its roots in the engineering colleges of India.

Today the Indian IT industry is gearing up to provide emerging technology solutions customized to the needs of their long-standing clients[39]. Compared to traditional IT-BPM projects, emerging technology projects are seen to provide better opportunities for engineers from non-IT specializations as these cater to different industrial sectors and firm contexts. In the case of AI, for example, the domain understanding that the non-IT engineers bring from their respective specializations can add substantial value while building use-case-centric AI solutions. These solutions are also seen to work better when the domain structure drives the implementation-specific activities[40]. A substantive engagement of non-IT engineers working in firm- or industry-specific AI use-cases can improve the accuracy of problem description, reduce the burden of data collection, and improve the model evaluation and interpretation[41].

For the Indian IT industry, this can be an opportunity to meaningfully engage with non-IT engineers beyond the usual software project requirements. It could help the Indian IT services organizations in particular to move up the client's value chain – a challenge we highlighted in the previous chapter. But, to facilitate that, we believe it is important for these organizations to recognize and mitigate the stark IT vs non-IT divide plaguing the emerging technology projects. Building appropriate workflows giving the necessary context and facilitating substantive engagement with data engineers, who come with the industry or firm's specific business domain, will definitely help. ITSO's research lab is working toward building AI-compatible workflows, and such efforts could be a first step toward enabling non-IT engineers to substantively engage with their domain expertise. In developing countries like India, where IT industry is the largest mobility pathway for engineers, this is critical to avoid wastage of the specialized skills with which millions of Indian engineers enter the workforce every year. That this realization has to also percolate down to the Indian engineering education system goes without saying.

Notes

1 Ramnath, A. (2017). The birth of an Indian profession: Engineers, industry, and the state, 1900–47. Oxford University Press.
2 Palit, S. K. (1998). The development of engineering and technical education in India. Government of India.
3 Bhargava, R. N. (2001). Present Engineering Education in India—An Emerging Economy—And a Glimpse of the Scenario in the 21st Century. In D. Weichert, B. Rauhut, & R. Schmidt (Eds.), Educating the Engineer for the 21st Century (pp. 77–80). Springer, Netherlands.
4 MHRD. (2003). Revitalizing Technical Education—Report on the review committee on AICTE. Ministry of Human Resource Development, Government of India.

5   Stremlau, J. (1996). Dateline Bangalore: Third world technopolis. Foreign Policy, 102, 152–168.
6   References: Balakrishnan, P. (2006). Benign neglect or strategic intent? Contested lineage of Indian software industry. Economic and Political Weekly, 3865–3872; Parthasarathy, B. (2004). India's Silicon Valley or Silicon Valley's India? Socially embedding the computer software industry in Bangalore. International Journal of Urban and Regional Research, 28(3), 664–685.
7   Fuller, C. J., & Narasimhan, H. (2007). Information technology professionals and the new-rich middle class in Chennai (Madras). Modern Asian Studies, 41(1), 121–150.
8   References: Jalote, P., & Natarajan, P. (2019). The growth and evolution of India's software industry. Communications of the ACM, 62(11), 64–69; Upadhya, C., & Vasavi, A. R. (2012). In an outpost of the global economy: Work and workers in India's information technology industry. Routledge.
9   References: Ramasubbu, N., Mithas, S., Krishnan, M. S., & Kemerer, C. F. (2008). Work dispersion, process-based learning, and offshore software development performance. MIS Quarterly, 437–458; Herbsleb, J. D. (2007). Global software engineering: The future of socio-technical coordination. Future of Software Engineering (FOSE'07), 188–198.
10 Arora, A., Arunachalam, V. S., Asundi, J., & Fernandes, R. (2001). The Indian software services industry. Research Policy, 30(8), 1267–1287.
11 Upadhya, C., & Vasavi, A. R. (2012). In an outpost of the global economy: Work and workers in India's information technology industry. Routledge.
12 Athreye, S. S. (2005). The Indian software industry and its evolving service capability. Industrial and Corporate Change, 14(3), 393–418.
13 Arora, A., Arunachalam, V. S., Asundi, J., & Fernandes, R. (2001). The Indian software services industry. Research Policy, 30(8), 1267–1287.
14 MHRD. (2015). Technical Education in India: A futuristic scenario, Report of the AICTE review committee, 2015. Ministry of Human Resource Development, Government of India.
15 World Bank. (2000). Scientific and Technical Manpower Development in India.
16 Ramarao, P. (1998). Reshaping postgraduate education and research in engineering and technology. Review Committee of the AICTE on PG Education in Research and Development in Engineering Technology, P126–127, Government of India.
17 Thakur, A., & Mantha, S. (2021). Modi Govt's HEC can't just be UGC with new label. Engineering still needs its own regulator.
18 Lasi, H., Fettke, P., Kemper, H.-G., Feld, T., & Hoffmann, M. (2014). Industry 4.0. Business & Information Systems Engineering, 6(4), 239–242.
19 NASSCOM. (2017). IT-BPM Strategic Review. National Association of Software and Service Companies.
20 Roy, M., & Roy, A. (2021). The rise of interdisciplinarity in engineering education in the era of industry 4.0: Implications for management practice. IEEE Engineering Management Review, 49(3), 56–70.
21 References: Taddy, M. (2019). The technological elements of artificial intelligence. University of Chicago Press, Chicago, IL; CMU, M. L. D. (2020, August 31). The Importance of Domain Knowledge. Machine Learning Blog, ML@CMU, Carnegie Mellon University. https://blog.ml.cmu.edu/2020/08/31/1-domain-knowledge/
22 Baruah, A. (2020). IT sector hiring in new-age skills to pick up in 2021. https://www.livemint.com. https://www.livemint.com/companies/news/it-sector-hiring-in-new-age-skills-to-pick-up-in-2021-11605686860932.html
23 NASSCOM. (2018). Talent Demand and Supply Report, AI and Big Data Analytics. National Association of Software and Service Companies.
24 For example: in legal/contractual documents, digitalization entails the need to extract contract elements such as names and addresses of entities involved in the contract, different types of clauses covered in the contract, etc.

25 Amershi, S., Begel, A., Bird, C., DeLine, R., Gall, H., Kamar, E., Nagappan, N., Nushi, B., & Zimmermann, T. (2019). Software engineering for machine learning: A case study. 2019 IEEE/ACM 41st International Conference on Software Engineering: Software Engineering in Practice (ICSE-SEIP), 291–300.

26 Amershi, S., Begel, A., Bird, C., DeLine, R., Gall, H., Kamar, E., Nagappan, N., Nushi, B., & Zimmermann, T. (2019). Software engineering for machine learning: A case study. 2019 IEEE/ACM 41st International Conference on Software Engineering: Software Engineering in Practice (ICSE-SEIP), 291–300.

27 Taddy, M. (2019). The technological elements of artificial intelligence. University of Chicago Press, Chicago, IL.

28 Agarwal, S. (2020). Layoffs: Allow surplus staff layoffs, flexible shifts: IT to states—The Economic Times. https://m.economictimes.com/tech/ites/allow-temp-sacking-of-staff-flexible-work-shifts-it-industry-to-states/amp_articleshow/76042143.cms

29 Camm, J., & Davenport, T. (2020). Data Science, Quarantined – MIT Sloan Management Review. https://sloanreview.mit.edu/article/data-science-quarantined/amp

30 Chawla, V. (2020). Are we seeing the data science bubble burst? Analytics India Magazine. https://analyticsindiamag.com/are-we-seeing-the-data-science-bubble-burst/

31 Roy, S. (2020). Pandemic proves to be a boon for Indian IT. Tribune India News Service. https://www.tribuneindia.com/news/comment/pandemic-proves-to-be-a-boon-for-indian-it-166070

32 Baruah, A. (2020). IT sector hiring in new-age skills to pick up in 2021. https://www.livemint.com. https://www.livemint.com/companies/news/it-sector-hiring-in-new-age-skills-to-pick-up-in-2021-11605686860932.html; Tavaga, R. (2020). Indian IT stocks on cloud 9! What next? Investing.Com India. https://in.investing.com/analysis/indian-it-stocks-on-cloud-9-what-next-200449643

33 Thakur, A., & Mantha, S. (2021). Modi Govt's HEC can't just be UGC with new label. Engineering still needs its own regulator.

34 An article based on our engineering college ethnographic study: Kamath, R., Venumuddala, V., & Manjunath, A. (2022). National Education Policy Needs to Strengthen Core Engineering Disciplines for the Success of Industry 4.0. https://www.forbesindia.com/article/iim-bangalore/national-education-policy-needs-to-strengthen-core-engineering-disciplines-for-the-success-of-industry-40/74023/1

35 Thakur, A., & Mantha, S. (2021). Modi Govt's HEC can't just be UGC with new label. Engineering still needs its own regulator.

36 NBA. (2019). National Board Accreditation Manual. National Board of Accreditation, Government of India.

37 Typically organized by the state university before undergraduate admissions.

38 These assignments form part of the college's internal assessment of students. Such internal assessments also carry some (less than 30%) weightage along with the main external examinations conducted by the state university, in determining a student's final grades.

39 NASSCOM. (2017). IT-BPM Strategic Review. National Association of Software and Service Companies.

40 Taddy, M. (2019). The technological elements of artificial intelligence. University of Chicago Press, Chicago, IL.

41 CMU, M. L. D. (2020, August 31). The Importance of Domain Knowledge. Machine Learning Blog. ML@CMU. Carnegie Mellon University. https://blog.ml.cmu.edu/2020/08/31/1-domain-knowledge/

5 Discussion

5.1 A summary of our findings

We have shown that given their historical relationship with clients across the globe, the Indian IT services organizations are in a better position to transition into the emerging technology space. They are rapidly garnering expertise around emerging technologies to address digital transformation needs of their clients. Digital transformation entails the integration of a client's value chain activities through emerging technologies, and takes the client's firm closer to, and being more responsive to, addressing the diverse needs of their customers. A substantive foray into digital transformation projects would require closer engagement by the service providers with activities at a relatively higher-end in the client's value chain, particularly integration and transformation of their core production and operational activities. Our study showed that, despite an avowed goal of becoming digital transformation solution providers, the Indian IT services organizations seem to be restricting themselves to a relatively lower-end of the clients' value chain. Their emerging technology research labs focus more on augmenting the mainstream client-focused IT and BPM services, to avoid becoming cost centers within their parent organizations. These IT-BPM services were traditionally meant to support non-core activities, such as customer relationship management (within marketing, sales, and service), human resource management (HRM), IT infrastructure management, and others, still at a relatively lower-end of the client's value chain. As a result of this need to avoid becoming a cost center, the workflows that they negotiate with clients for emerging technology projects, tend to be heavily influenced by the workflows associated with their traditional IT-BPM projects. As per our ethnographic findings in the Artificial Intelligence (AI) research lab, these negotiated workflows only end up sustaining emerging technology work at the lower-end of client's value chain. Although they might anticipate value addition to client's core production and operational activities, such projects are likely to end up as a research activity only.

IT giants, like Google, Microsoft, IBM, Amazon, and so on, are innovating not just in IT but in the space of emerging technologies like AI, Cloud,

DOI: 10.1201/9781003324355-5

Internet of Things (IoT), Blockchain, and so on. With a first-mover advantage, they have built platforms and products, many of which have turned out to be foundational to a vast array of emerging technology solutions now being adopted by individuals and firms across the globe. These Big-Tech companies are therefore present at the higher-end of the emerging technology value chain. Indian IT services organizations rely heavily on the generic platforms and products developed by these companies. In the context of our study, we have seen that ITSO and IT service organizations like it, rely on cloud platforms, like Azure, Amazon Web Services, and Machine learning platforms like Google's TensorFlow, to build client-centric AI solutions. Organizations like ITSO have the wherewithal to scale up the emerging technology value chain by building IPs that can be later on customized for their different clients. But the workflows that they negotiate with their long-standing clients affect this potential for innovations at the higher-end of the emerging technology product value chain.

IT services organizations operating from India have a distinct comparative advantage in the sheer volume of skilled workforce that they accommodate. This workforce is trained in diverse engineering disciplines, and also more recently, in basic and applied Sciences. With this scale and variety of available talent, there is a lot of scope for the IT services organizations to move up the emerging technology value chain and make contributions in technology stack solutions at a more foundational level, akin to the global IT giants. To make this happen, the IT services organizations will need to address the mobility constraints facing their workforce, in particular the constraints of those engineers coming with non-IT backgrounds.

Our study indicated a visible mobility constraint for engineers, especially for those from non-IT disciplines who aspired toward emerging technology roles in the space of AI. Paradoxically, compared to the traditional software and business process services, emerging technology solutions were expected to provide better opportunities for engineers from non-IT backgrounds as these solutions need to be tailor-made for different industrial sectors and firm contexts. Domain expertise of such engineers can be helpful in better eliciting the client's business use-cases falling in a similar domain. For example, mechanical engineers can engage much more deeply with automobile and manufacturing contexts and elicit emerging technology use-cases that could be far more optimal and foundational to the auto and manufacturing industry. Similarly, civil engineers can engage with construction and structural design use-cases. So also, electrical engineers could engage with smart grid use-cases in the power sector. Since these engineers are already being equipped with IT and emerging technology skillsets in the IT services organizations, their engagement with domain-centered client use-cases can help these organizations make contributions to industry-specific technology stacks in the emerging technology space. However, to make this happen, there is a need to renegotiate workflows with clients so that such engineers, while occupying their respective technical roles, can also be exposed to the client's business domain and use-cases. Similarly, to make the most of prospective non–IT engineers, there is a need to incorporate IT and emerging technology modules into their academic curriculum so that they can contribute more meaningfully to the IT industry as it transitions toward offering digital transformation solutions to clients across industries.

5.2 Relooking client-vendor relationships in the Indian IT sector

The Indian IT sector is globally acclaimed for providing offshore-outsourcing projects in the space of IT software and Business Process Management (BPM). Offshoring helped clients to focus on their core business activities, which was an essential requirement to sustain competition[1]. Adherence to standard workflows, client-specific investments around infrastructure, personnel training, etc., we some critical factors that turned the Indian IT service providers into highly preferred offshore destinations for clients[2]. The client-vendor relationships in this sector saw the Indian IT organizations moving from offering simple coding services to taking up design and development of custom software for clients. Indian IT organizations also moved from providing low-end BPM services, such as call center and back-office work to offering high-value customer interaction services, and customization of enterprises planning systems for their clients[3]. Service exports from the IT-BPM segment of the Indian IT industry contributes to a staggering 38% of the total services exports of the country[4].

Our research was around this new era unfolding for the Indian IT services organizations undertaking offshore emerging technology projects for their long-standing clients. Our key findings highlighted the repercussions of incompatible workflows on these emerging technology projects and on the mobility of engineers, working in these projects. We pointed out very specifically, a need for the Indian IT services organizations to negotiate compatible workflows with their clients. But this negotiation has to be seen in the wider context of existing client-vendor relationships and has to avoid disrupting the long-standing nature of client-vendor relationships in the Indian IT sector. A relook into how the client-vendor relationships will unfold in this new era is thus, called for. Although a full-fledged picture on this is beyond the scope of this work, our ethnographic study provides some pointers into this newly evolving client-vendor relationships where clients are offshoring emerging technology projects to Indian IT service providers – like ITSO. We discuss these insights in the following subsections.

5.2.1 Influence of clients on the nature of emerging technology work

At ITSO, the majority of the AI projects are concerned with the augmentation of clients' offshored IT-BPM services. Automating some manual tasks within such software and business process services drives down the costs for clients and helps them deal with attrition issues[5]. Clients often offshore both the IT-BPM services and the AI projects concerning their automation, to a single service provider. For the Indian IT services organizations, this scenario leads to a tight-rope walk – they have to fulfill clients' requirements by automating manual work of their own offshore development workers, leading to their job losses. In ITSO's AI research lab, there are differing opinions expressed by the team members about this possibility. For some, offshore AI projects leading to job losses are a reality and could destroy the main selling point for the Indian IT services organizations – which is their skilled offshore workers. For instance, Sruthi, a senior data scientist, opines about this as follows.

> *clients ask for AI solutions to IT-BPM companies … although IT-BPM companies work towards building such solutions and integrating it with the BPM services, like this team does, it's actually in contradiction to the original selling point of companies like this … employee count or resource count is what makes IT service companies attractive for managing client business processes, now if AI solutions attempt to automate the work of many employees, then is it not counter-productive strategy for these companies?*

Other contrasting opinions, especially those held by the key managerial roles in the Lab, dominate. For example, Kamal, the business analyst, downplays the intensity of job losses due to offshore AI projects.

> *The cost reduction by virtue of adopting AI technology … is only to replace the manual execution with automated execution. Despite AI based automation, manual tasks may not completely come down because of the uncertainty in the accuracy of task execution by the AI models. Some amount of manual work, however less than what was present earlier, nevertheless exists.*

In our previous chapters, we have seen that the execution of AI projects at ITSO was heavily influenced by the traditional workflows of IT-BPM projects – which were convenient to clients as they facilitated clear division of tasks and billability. Such workflows limited the ITSO's scope for innovation in the emerging technology space, particularly AI. In addition, the above ethnographic observations point to another important influence of clients, i.e., on the kind of AI projects that may get offshored to Indian service providers in the first place. In essence, at the negotiation table, we find that clients could have an upper hand in dictating the kind of emerging technology work undertaken by the Indian IT services organizations.

5.2.2 Negotiating factors for a newly evolving client-vendor relationships

Clients typically have the freedom to switch between several vendors that are available in the offshore-outsourcing arena. However, literature notes that the client-vendor relationships in the context of IT-BPM services is predominantly a long term one and its strength is dependent upon both client-side and vendor-side factors[6]. Some important client-side factors include – (a) client-specific investments made in software, infrastructure, and personnel training by the vendors, (b) vendors gaining sufficient specialized knowledge around client's businesses and their corresponding industry verticals, and (c) clients given greater scope for monitoring and control over the offshore work taken up by the vendor[7]. On the other hand, some important vendor-side factors include – (a) well-defined time and scope of routine projects, and time to adjust work processes in case of new technology projects and (b) minimizing attrition of employees working in the offshore projects. The former are particularly vital for the vendors to build generic workflows that can accommodate the diversity of their clientele. In case of new technology projects, this means that vendors will be better off when clients acknowledge relevant process adjustments to avoid cost or time overruns. Minimizing employee attrition is crucial to the vendors as the offshore workers are the prime reason for the attractiveness of the Indian IT services organizations like ITSO[8].

Our ethnographic observations indicate that there is a greater weightage given to the client-side factors in the newly evolving client-vendor relationships of the emerging technology era. This is evident through the overwhelming influence of clients on the nature of emerging technology work taken up by the offshore service providers and the client-specific investments being made by the vendors in terms of trading off innovation for client-focused customization of emerging technology projects. Vendor-side factors seem to have taken a back seat as we saw in the case of incompatible workflows, and the possibility of job losses of offshore workers given the nature of emerging technology projects being taken up. At ITSO's AI research lab, we see that there are some efforts in the context of the former. The AI-specific workflow adjustments are being experimented at this lab, and efforts are on to educate clients to acknowledge and understand AI-specific peculiarities in offshore projects. However, the efforts toward tackling job losses of the offshore workers are currently lacking.

We believe that vendors – like the Indian IT services organizations – need to pay considerable attention to vendor-specific developments that can add strength to their relationship with clients. In case of emerging technology projects, our study highlights that (a) educating clients to seek reasonable time and space for building emerging technology-compatible workflows and (b) incorporating measures to tackle possible job losses of their offshore workers could be vital for the Indian IT services organizations to act upon. The longevity of client-vendor relationships in the era of emerging technologies can be guaranteed only when vendors duly acknowledge the importance of taking concrete steps in this direction.

5.3 Implications of this study to the Indian IT industry and policy

5.3.1 India's IT-led innovations and the road ahead

In the IT space, India is slowly gearing up toward creating foundational technological stacks, many of which have now become enablers for a plethora of digital services for its citizens and small businesses. It is getting global acclaim for its digitalization initiatives around personal identity, payments, taxation, and the more recent data-sharing systems. In the context of identity, the Unique Identification Authority of India (UIDAI) established an identity authentication ecosystem to effectively enable service delivery to its citizens anywhere in the country. Over 90% of the citizens now have this unique identity number called Aadhaar and it has become a widely accepted and verifiable identity for service providers across banking and other domains in the country[9]. The digital ecosystem enabled by UIDAI facilitates instant Know Your Customer (KYC) norms for banks to verify the identity of an individual. This is helping citizens to open bank accounts faster than before and with less hassle. Aadhaar is also smoothening the provision of citizen-centric government services such as direct benefit transfers, LPG gas subsidies, passport issues, disbursement of provident funds, etc. Although contested for the data security and privacy concerns, the evolvability inbuilt within its digital ecosystem gives scope for their eventual resolution. In any case, being a minimalistic, context-free, unique, and verifiable identity, there is a widespread agreement among stakeholders within business, government, and society that Aadhaar is a foundational welfare-enabling instrument of the state. It is simplifying the identity verification process when services are increasingly moving online. Reduced cost of identity verification is streamlining the distribution of welfare benefits to its citizens and is also facilitating the large migratory population to better participate in the economy. Overall, Aadhaar is finely balancing an evolutionary solution prioritizing the short-term needs of India's poor vs a theoretically perfect solution prioritizing the security and privacy concerns[10].

The Aadhaar identity system has also become a central piece for another foundational technology stack in India – the Unified Payments Interface (UPI). UPI and its underpinning digital payments infrastructure have facilitated cashless peer-to-peer or peer-to-merchant transactions. The digital infrastructure setup by the National Payments Corporation of India[11] enabled the well-known payment service providers, like Google Pay, PhonePe, PayTM, and many more, to facilitate such transactions. An unprecedented rise in the usage of these apps was witnessed during the COVID-19 pandemic not just for their facility of cash-less transactions but also for their touch-free experience[12]. Today UPI has become pervasive and has reached to the remotest parts of the country wherever there is at least a mobile Internet connectivity.

For informal small businesses, UPI is acknowledged to be a highly supportive instrument as it makes their financial transactions with customers less difficult. Focusing on their core activities is now easier. Another digital platform for India's context-specific needs is the e-filing Income tax platform that is built by Infosys, a well-known Indian IT services organization. This platform promises ease of use to taxpayers to file their returns, provides access to their previous returns, minimizes errors in the filing entries, maintains confidentiality of their tax records, and most importantly hastens the overall process of income tax filing. Despite initial glitches, the platform was eventually successful in achieving its stated purpose. For the financial year 2020–2021, over 3 crore taxpayers have filed their income tax returns through this portal[13].

The more recent common technology framework for data sharing and empowerment is led by the Reserve Bank of India, its central bank. It is a global first and envisages an interoperable platform for consented data sharing between individuals or small businesses and any financial institution in the country. This is expected to be a basis for a new fintech revolution in India-specific product and services innovations around flow-based lending, financial management, etc[14]. All the aforementioned technology innovations founded in India are becoming basis for many startups in the country. These technology stacks are now playing a role akin to what the platforms developed by Big-Tech companies have done to usher the growth of several other companies – examples being the cab-share platforms Ola and Uber relying on Google Maps. More such IT-based foundational stacks are being developed in India in the space of open e-commerce[15], distributed ledger platforms[16], and so on.

The present IT-led innovations that India is witnessing are commendable and owe a lot to the talented workforce that the IT services industry, with its growth and promise of mobility, has attracted over the past four decades. However, there is still a long way to go when it comes to transforming other sectors, especially the primary and secondary sectors – agriculture-related and manufacturing. Innovations in the areas of clean energy, water management, waste management, transportation, environmental sustainability, etc. are the need of the hour as many Indian cities are now being pushed to their limits in terms of governance in these areas[17]. IT-led innovations will play a major role in transforming these sectors. Platform-based innovations in the area of shared mobility being one example. However, to have these technological innovations meaningfully transform these areas, a combination of emerging technologies and respective sectoral or domain expertise becomes crucial. An organizational culture where domain experts are called upon to proactively engage in the design, implementation, and usage of their domain-specific IT or emerging technology solutions is vital to the long-term sustainability of such solutions[18]. To drive home, the points discussed above, we highlight in Box 5.1, an example of the domain-specific complexities that one needs to engage with while building a digital platform that connects various stakeholders in building a sustainable smart electricity grid.

Box 5.1

Problem facing electricity distribution utilities in India

Large-scale adoption of distributed energy resources (DERs), such as roof-top solar installations, battery storage systems, electric vehicles, micro and mini grids, etc., is considered important for achieving carbon emission reduction targets set by a country[19]. To achieve this scale, there is a need to transition from the relatively inflexible top-down traditional electricity grid to a flexible smart grid, through the incorporation of necessary information and communication technologies[20]. The key objectives of any smart grid are (a) consumer participation in the overall energy management, (b) rapid integration of renewable energy sources into the supply, (c) peak power reduction, and (d) efficient grid management through grid modernization[21]. Transition to smart grid is fraught with problems in India, particularly at the levels of power distribution and consumption. Although the Electricity Act, 2003, paves way for private players to enter into the space of electricity distribution, 90% of the population of the country is still served by state-owned distribution companies or utilities. The long-term Power Purchase Agreements (PPAs) that these utilities enter with the upstream bulk energy suppliers have resulted in the average cost of energy supply being consistently higher than the state-regulated retail energy tariffs, leading to serious losses for the utilities[22]. Distribution utilities are therefore slow to conduct grid modernization activities. The inefficient retail energy tariffs also disincentivize individual households to adopt DERs like roof-top solar (due to low-price of the grid electricity). Utility companies are also slow to approve them without incurring a loss for themselves[23]. Therefore, the difficult problem that has to be resolved through a smart grid is to enable utilities to reduce their operational costs and modernize the grid and at the same time encourage consumers to adopt DERs. Else, this could lead to a vicious cycle, termed as the utility death spiral, where consumers – in particular the industrial high-value consumers – go off-grid, pushing utilities into more and more losses and eventual collapse[24].

Aggregator platform

Aggregators are considered to be important in resolving this difficult problem in the context of a transition to sustainable energy[25]. They can build the necessary digital platforms where consumers can buy or sell renewable power through their DERs in retail energy markets, and where utilities can transact with an aggregated set of consumers through the aggregator platform and better manage their upstream supply contracts. An aggregator platform can also facilitate grid-stabilizing ancillary services by appropriately aggregating predictable energy sources or loads in the downstream, and offer them as levers for the utility to effectively match demand and supply. This way, aggregator platforms can create a win-win situation for both utilities and the consumers. For utilities, it can help to move from long-term PPAs to short-term contracts with the upstream bulk energy suppliers. Ancillary services can help utilities to reduce their operational costs. Aggregators can offer price incentives to consumers so that they could plan

(*Continued*)

Box 5.1 (*Continued*)

the usage of their dispatchable loads[26] to save their energy bills. They also facilitate retail energy markets where consumers can sell their excess power generated from DERs (like roof-top solar) at a reasonable price quoted offered by other consumers located in a similar zone. From a policy point of view this can help in tackling the rising carbon foot-print by (a) reducing the need for excess fossil-fuel-based energy generation, which is expected in the current regime of long-term PPA-based contracts that utilities enter into with the upstream bulk energy producers and (b) scaling the renewable energy adoption by incentivizing not only industrial but also individual consumers to uptake DERs.

Domain-specific technology complexity

The kind of aggregator-based digital platforms discussed above help utilities to conduct demand-response programs for its end consumers. Under such programs, utilities can incentivize consumers based on their energy consumption patterns. Typically, smart meters are installed for this purpose at the consumer locations so that their ongoing consumption patterns are relayed in real time to the utility. With the mediating platform, consumers can also promise utilities about the load/capacity they can adjust in the ensuing forecast horizon (like day-ahead, week-ahead, or month-ahead), so that utilities can plan their upstream contracts accordingly. Even without a consumer's active feedback, machine learning-based applications are usually employed by the utilities to assess such forecasts for minimizing their upstream costs[27]. Utilities also leverage dispatchable loads of a set of consumers through the aggregator platform to maintain grid stability. Since energy supply-demand matching has to happen extremely close to real time, the dynamism of such platforms and their reliability must meet very tight criteria. In its absence, it could result in unmanageable blackouts that can cause severe economic loss and even loss of lives[28]. Therefore, the reliability and responsiveness of such platforms will depend upon the underlying electrical and electronics infrastructure associated with the generation, transmission, distribution, and consumption components in the energy supply chain. Same applies to the reliability of IoT sensors deployed to collect information at different components in the energy supply chain. Blockchain-based smart contracts, if at all conceived as an alternative to aggregator platforms, will again depend upon these domain-specific complexities. Whether it be IoT systems for aggregating sensor-generated information from different components of an energy system, or AI systems for forecasting consumption and generation schedules, or IT platforms or Blockchain-based decentralized platforms for enabling retail energy markets, the fact that a tremendous domain-specific complexity drives their development is indisputable. Emerging technology solutions in smart grid need to be carried out in unison with other engineering components within the system. Therefore, the engagement of domain experts (could be electrical engineers or power system engineers) who are also skilled in emerging technologies will be extremely helpful in the context of their design and deployment.

5.3.2 Can the Indian IT services industry unleash its abundant domain expertise?

As we saw in the context of our study, Indian IT services organizations also attract workforce from non-IT disciplinary backgrounds. Apart from MBA graduates, who enter into managerial roles with expertise in domains like finance, marketing, sales, or human resources management, engineering graduates from non-IT backgrounds such as mechanical, electrical, electronics, and civil engineering enter at the beginner or entry-level roles in large numbers and their employability is measured by their expertise in software development[29]. Despite the diversity of skills present in their workforce, IT services organizations continue to train their engineers around software development since that is their mainstay. Our study points to a growing opportunity for these organizations to utilize the industry-specific domain expertise of their non-IT engineers, who come with a rigorous training in these fields in their four years of engineering. This opportunity has arisen because of the digital transformation expectations from clients, which has triggered the need for building in-house expertise in emerging technologies to offer client-focused customized solutions. We believe that a deeper engagement of non-IT engineers with clients' core value chain activities can sharpen their unexplored domain expertise and help IT services organizations to offer industry-specific digital transformation solutions higher up the value chain. In a similar vein, unleashing the capability of a majority of non-IT workforce could also mean that the IT services industry, the largest private sector employer of the country, can engage with the country's pressing problems – like clean energy, sustainable transport, water management, so on – across industry verticals. The capabilities of their workforce in terms of having domain-specific skills and expertise around IT and emerging technology solutions could help the IT industry to contribute toward more foundational innovations in the emerging technology space and across sectors of the country.

Currently, there are conscious policy efforts to prepare the Indian IT industry for emerging technology-driven future industrial transformation, particularly steering them toward the country's own requirements and its contextual specificities. For example, the National Policy on software products[30], 2019, has been announced recently to provide a conducive ecosystem for helping the Indian IT industry, which is currently services-led, to move up the value chain to the products segment. By providing access to finance through dedicated funds and budgetary outlays, it intends to promote product-based start-ups which can keep this industry at pace with the advancement of emerging technologies like AI, IoT, Blockchain, and so on. By promoting innovation in software and emerging technology products' space, this policy also envisages sector-specific technology solutions that can unleash the untapped growth potential even from other indigenous industries beyond IT. In the context of such policies, we opine that too much reliance on start-ups for driving software or emerging technology solutions for India's needs might lead to missing out on the skills and expertise of a large and existing workforce in established IT services organizations.

How can the IT services organizations unleash the true potential of their workforce, particularly of their non-IT domain experts? From our ethnographic study, we find that a structural change within such organizations is required to make this happen. Our study has shown that despite venturing into the emerging technology space, the current workflows that such organizations negotiate with clients are heavily aligned with the workflows of their traditional software and BPM projects. Such workflows aim at fine-tuning the task division between engineers, enabling them to work independently and in relative isolation from others. These workflows are not compatible with the emerging technology work where activities are too entangled and complex to be able to be clearly separated and assigned to different roles. We observed that the non–IT data engineers (beginner roles) working in the AI space faced mobility constraints where they were unable to transpose the skills for which they were recruited – data sciences and operations management – and had to cope with software engineering work in which they had limited expertise. Their work context, dominated by software workflows, made it difficult for them to engage deeply with clients' actual business activities from where the AI use-cases were elicited. Despite their specialized skills to contribute in such a space, they continued to work with software programming tasks that were assigned to them during the project. We believe that companies should not fight shy about revisiting the new workflows being negotiated with clients in the context of emerging technology projects. Only when such workflows enable deeper engagement of domain experts (even at their beginner roles) in the client's business activities, innovations can happen at the higher-end of the value chain – whether it be the client's value chain or the emerging technology value chain.

Our study also has something to say to the HRM functionaries, managers and the team leads in the Indian IT organizations. Managers and the human resource practitioners play a crucial role in managing the workforce for different client projects in the IT services organizations. Their actions toward the betterment of their employees are often targeted and individual-specific, such as setting standards in identifying laggards and achievers, boosting employee motivation, and managing compliance and grievance issues. The underlying ethos is that project timelines and deadlines are sacrosanct. A customary answer to a lot of these workplace issues is sought in a combination of sticks and carrots – an underlying threat of pink slips along with seminars on employee motivation, upskilling training, salary hikes, bonuses, and promises of onsite work. The assumption being that these tools help employees cope with their high-pressure job demands, tackle a stressful environment, and navigate cultural differences, especially in globally distributed environments like the Indian software services industry[31]. While there could be benefits to adopting such individualistic employee-focused tools, our study highlights the importance of a deeper engagement with the technological and organizational structures affecting work. It is widely acknowledged that role clarity is an important constituent of mature process workflows to ensure distributed software development work[32]. Socio-technical interventions, like negotiating emerging technology-compatible workflows, could widen the scope of work for the beginner roles in the emerging technology space. We saw that the disillusionment of data engineers in the lab in terms of mismatched expectations vs reality got further exacerbated in distributed environments scenario of Work from Home (WFH). Our study indicates that such socio-technical interventions, such as ensuring compatible project workflows, enriching context awareness, and building necessary clarity for different work roles will be a prerequisite for such employee-focused management tools to work in the context of emerging technology projects like that of AI. This also allows a more meaningful transposition of their otherwise underutilized domain-specific disciplinary skillsets, thereby facilitating a healthy career progression. Such interventions might also be necessary for the employee-focused management tools to succeed in the long term and solve the problem of attrition that the Indian IT services industry is currently grappling with[33].

5.3.3 Implications to industrial and educational policy

India's sectoral growth is often characterized by a premature movement of its workforce toward the services industry, bypassing the manufacturing or secondary sector[34], which has witnessed a relative stagnation or decline in the past decades[35]. The rapid growth of Indian IT services industry and its position as the largest private sector employer in the country also signifies this, especially for the skilled workforce such as engineers. Entry of the engineers from non-IT disciplinary backgrounds into the IT industry has meant that, with their transformation into generic software engineers and programmers, there was an underutilization of their disciplinary specialized skillsets. We surmise that this disengagement from their specialized (non-IT) disciplinary skillsets by large number of engineers, who get pulled into IT services organizations, could perhaps be an important but neglected reason for the relative stagnation or decline of India's secondary sector. With the transition of the Indian IT industry toward emerging technologies, our study shows that the same industry could now contribute toward a relatively better engagement of non-IT engineers in their respective disciplinary specializations in the industry. These engineers could set in motion industry-specific innovations around digital transformation that could trigger growth in other industries within the secondary sector. It is possible to usher context-specific digital transformation solutions for India's indigenous industry, particularly in the informal and SME segment. Channelizing these efforts of non-IT engineers, or other domain experts in general, might require appropriate policy directives for India's IT sector. How to get the established IT services organizations to engage their domain experts in the indigenization of emerging technologies is, therefore, a big policy conundrum that policymakers need to resolve while devising any such incentives.

The need for domain or industry-specific skillsets is now becoming important for the emerging technology work roles in the IT services industry far more than in the past. As emerging technologies are expected to drive industry transformation in all industry verticals, we believe that demand for such work roles might increase in the future, even in sectors other than the IT. From a supply side, our study shows that the majority of the engineering colleges in the country seem to be disproportionately aligning their organizational structures and processes in placing their prospective engineers in the IT industry. This is leading to a gradual decline in the significance of the traditional non-IT engineering disciplines like mechanical engineering, civil engineering, electrical engineering, and others[36]. India's new educational policy aims to facilitate greater academic autonomy to these colleges so that they could better adjust to the industry expectations[37]. But there is a lurking danger of a further neglect of the non-IT engineering disciplines by laying greater emphasis on IT or purely emerging-technology-based disciplines. From an educational policy perspective, there is a need to tackle this neglect by promoting and regulating interdisciplinarity, where non-IT engineering disciplines are exposed to IT and emerging technology courses. The aim should be to have the engineering graduates industry ready – whether it be for the sector-specific emerging technology work in the IT industry or in their discipline-specific industries.

5.4 Conclusion and future work

Our study points to a possibility for the Indian IT services organizations engaging in activities higher up their client's value chain and shows how their in-house domain experts – specifically, the non-IT engineers – can become a crucial advantage in this endeavor. Increasingly, India is witnessing a state-driven or state-supported in-house technology stack development not just in IT but other emerging technologies. We believe that the Indian IT services industry, by engaging at the higher-end of value chain can garner expertise that could enable them to make significant contributions to the more foundational layers of these technology stacks in the space of emerging technologies. Unleashing the potential of its workforce and its diversity of specializations will be the key to realizing this. Therefore, for the managers and human resource managers in this industry, it is important to look at renegotiation of workflows with the clients, particularly to make them compatible with building context-specific emerging technology solutions. From a policy perspective, this can be a game-changer for the country. The Indian industry could be in a place to enable foundational technology stacks suiting the specific firm (e.g., SMEs) and industry contexts in the country. From an educational policy point of view, there is a dire need to substantively integrate emerging technology modules into the curriculum of non-IT engineering disciplines, and if possible other disciplines wherever relevant. Engagement of domain experts in the emerging technology space to solve specific industrial problems will help in a balanced sectoral development of the country.

The scope of our study is defined by the organization we studied and the extensions or plausible generalizations that we could make. Our findings related to emerging technology project workflows, and mobility prospects of engineers working in the beginner roles, may have lessons for the global capability centers of Big-Tech firms and other product-based multinational firms, and product-based IT or emerging technology startups, given the country-specific context in which they find themselves. IT services organizations operating from India are undoubtedly the dominant players in the Indian IT industry and attract skilled workforce, particularly engineers, disproportionately greater than any other industry in the country. Although their transition toward emerging technologies is relatively new, our study shows that this transition is heavily influenced by the historically driven relationship between the IT services industry and its long-standing clients. Such a transition is also situated within the policy ecosystem of the country which allowed a flourishing of IT services organizations through appropriate incentives, and also led to a mushrooming of private engineering colleges which became the dominant suppliers of workforce to such organizations. Therefore, in generalizing our findings to IT service providers of other countries, care should be taken to point out the difference in the industry and policy environments and how they could affect such organizations and their transition toward emerging technologies. We believe these limitations can motivate future research work around empirical studies in similar organizations in other countries.

Notes

1 Oza, N. V. (2006). An empirical evaluation of client-vendor relationships in Indian software outsourcing companies. School of Computer Science.

2 References: Cusumano, M., MacCormack, A., Kemerer, C. F., & Crandall, B. (2003). Software development worldwide: The state of the practice. IEEE Software, 20(6), 28–34; Jalote, P., & Natarajan, P. (2019). The growth and evolution of India's software industry. Communications of the ACM, 62(11), 64–69.

3 NASSCOM. (2017). IT-BPM Strategic Review. National Association of Software and Service Companies.

4 MEITY. (2017). Fact Sheet of IT & BPM Industry | Ministry of Electronics and Information Technology, Government of India. Retrieved January 26, 2021, from https://www.meity.gov.in/content/fact-sheet-it-bpm-industry

5 In this regard a project manager in the AI research lab recounts his understanding, *"attrition is high … people get 1- or 1.5-years' experience and then move to [other] company … problem they [client's team] said is that when they [workforce part of the process] leave, they take away lot of tacit knowledge along with them, and the new ones take lot of time in ramping up to this knowledge … tacit knowledge helps [them] to easily fill in some information without googling … [client's] productivity is going down because of this employee attrition."*

6   References: Manning, S., Lewin, A. Y., & Schuerch, M. (2011). The stability of offshore outsourcing relationships. Management International Review, 51(3), 381–406; Rajkumar, T. M., & Mani, R. V. S. (2001). Offshore software development. Information Systems Management, 18(2), 63–74.

7   Manning, S., Lewin, A. Y., & Schuerch, M. (2011). The stability of offshore outsourcing relationships. Management International Review, 51(3), 381–406.

8   Rajkumar, T. M., & Mani, R. V. S. (2001). Offshore software development. Information Systems Management, 18(2), 63–74.

9   Press Trust of India. (2020, March 19). Aadhaar Cards issued to over 90% population of India as of Feb 2020: Govt. Business Standard India. https://www.business-standard.com/article/pti-stories/aadhaar-issued-to-over-90-pc-of-population-dhotre-120031901006_1.html

10 Eaves, D., & Goldberg, D. Aadhar—India's Big Experiment with Unique Identification, Case Study from Harvard Kennedy School.

11 NPCI acts as a trusted switch connecting banks and payment service providers. It is a non-profit organization setup by the Reserve Bank of India and is also funded by major banks in the country.

12 Business Line. (2021). The technology-led payments revolution. https://www.thehindubusinessline.com/opinion/the-payments-revolution/article34416453.ece

13 Infosys. (2021). Over 3 crore Taxpayers Successfully Complete Transactions. 1.5 crore Income Tax Returns Filed. https://www.infosys.com/newsroom/press-releases/2021/further-streamlining-end-user-experience.html

14 Chandra, K. (2019, December 6). A Great Leap Forward to Transform Fintech: Data Empowerment. ProductNation. https://pn.ispirt.in/a-great-leap-forward-to-transform-fintech-data-empowerment/

15 Beckn. (2022, March 11). Enabling Trusted Commerce using Beckn Protocol and Blockchain. Beckn Protocol. https://becknprotocol.io/enabling-trusted-commerce-using-beckn-protocol-and-blockchain/

16 Phadke, S. (2022, January 24). Bharat Distributed Ledger (BADAL) for accelerating trusted commerce in India. ProductNation. https://pn.ispirt.in/badal-for-accelerating-commerce-in-india/

17 Raj, P. (n.d.). Forbes India— - Transparency, Participation, and Accountability: Three Ways to Fix Indian Cities. Forbes India. Retrieved May 19, 2022, from https://www.forbesindia.com/article/iim-bangalore/transparency-participation-and-accountability-three-ways-to-fix-indian-cities/71811/1

18 UNESCO. (2021). Recommendation on the Ethics of Artificial Intelligence.

19 Poudineh, R., Mukherjee, M., & Elizondo, G. (2021). The rise of distributed energy resources: A case study of India's power market. OIES Paper: EL.

20 Rivas, A. E. L., & Abrao, T. (2020). Faults in smart grid systems: Monitoring, detection and classification. Electric Power Systems Research, 189, 106602.

21 Budka, K. C., Deshpande, J. G., & Thottan, M. (2016). Communication networks for smart grids. Springer.

22 NITI Aayog. (2021). Turning Around the Power Distribution Sector: Learnings and Best Practices from Reforms.

23 Poudineh, R., Mukherjee, M., & Elizondo, G. (2021). The rise of distributed energy resources: A case study of India's power market. OIES Paper: EL.

24 Castaneda, M., Jimenez, M., Zapata, S., Franco, C. J., & Dyner, I. (2017). Myths and facts of the utility death spiral. Energy Policy, 110, 105–116.

25 Burger, S., Chaves-Ávila, J. P., Batlle, C., & Pérez-Arriaga, I. J. (2017). A review of the value of aggregators in electricity systems. Renewable and Sustainable Energy Reviews, 77, 395–405.

26 Dispatchable loads are those which the consumers can change at least a portion of their consumption within a stipulated interval upon instruction from the utility. See: https://en.wikipedia.org/wiki/Dispatchable_generation

27 Krishnadas, G., & Kiprakis, A. (2020). A machine learning pipeline for demand response capacity scheduling. Energies, 13(7), 1848.

28 https://en.wikipedia.org/wiki/2021_Texas_power_crisis

29 Infotech. (2017). 95% engineers in India unfit for software development jobs: Study. https://www.thehindubusinessline.com/info-tech/95-engineers-in-india-unfit-for-software-development-jobs-study/article9652211.ece

30 https://www.meity.gov.in/writereaddata/files/national_policy_on_software_products-2019.pdf

31 Adamovic, M. (2018). An employee-focused human resource management perspective for the management of global virtual teams. The International Journal of Human Resource Management, 29(14), 2159–2187; Agrawal, N. M., Khatri, N., & Srinivasan, R. (2012). Managing growth: Human resource management challenges facing the Indian software industry. Journal of World Business, 47(2), 159–166.

32 Herbsleb, J. D., & Mockus, A. (2003). An empirical study of speed and communication in globally distributed software development. IEEE Transactions on Software Engineering, 29(6), 481–494; Ramasubbu, N., Mithas, S., Krishnan, M. S., & Kemerer, C. F. (2008). Work dispersion, process-based learning, and offshore software development performance. MIS Quarterly, 437–458; Yilmaz, M., O'Connor, R. V., & Clarke, P. (2012). A systematic approach to the comparison of roles in the software development processes. International Conference on Software Process Improvement and Capability Determination, 198–209. Springer.

33 Singh, A. (2022). Indian IT industry battling all-time high attrition rate. The Week. https://www.theweek.in/news/biz-tech/2022/05/19/indian-it-industry-battling-all-time-high-attrition-rate.html

34 Lamba, R., & Subramanian, A. (2020). Dynamism with incommensurate development: The distinctive Indian model. Journal of Economic Perspectives, 34(1), 3–30.

35 Basu, K., & Maertens, A. (2007). The pattern and causes of economic growth in India. Oxford Review of Economic Policy, 23(2), 143–167.

36 AICTE. (2018). Engineering Education in India: Short- and Medium-Term perspectives. All India Council for Technical Education, Government of India.

37 New Education Policy 2020, Ministry of Human Resource Development, Government of India., https://www.education.gov.in/sites/upload_files/mhrd/files/NEP_Final_English_0.pdf

Theoretical appendix

A.1 Critical realism: The philosophical basis

The philosophical basis of our work is the meta-theoretical framework called Critical Realism (CR). It states our commitment to a philosophical position that steers clear of the two classic binaries found in most social science research today: (i) the positivist paradigm that deals with regularities, law-like causalities, and regression-based models and (ii) the interpretivist paradigm that deals only with subjective interpretations and descriptions of social phenomena[1]. CR situates itself as an alternative paradigm to both these and owes its initial formulation to the works of Roy Bhaskar (1944–2014), the English philosopher of science[2]. Its basic tenet is that, unlike the natural world, the social world is intrinsically not a closed system and therefore the methodologies of natural sciences are inapplicable to the social sciences. This makes for an impossibility of experiments in the social sciences, where closed systems do not spontaneously occur and nor can they be artificially created. Thus, the rational assessment of any social phenomenon cannot be predictive but has to be explanatory. However, this does not jettison the researchers' obligations to be scientific in their explanations. They cannot take recourse to the interpretivist stance that social phenomena are products of individual beliefs and actions that can only be interpreted and described. That is because at the heart of CR is the belief (ontology) that social phenomena, very much like natural phenomena, are real, and just not in the subjective minds of actors. This premise, called *ontological reality*, makes critical realists insist on the reality of social events and discourses and explains the realism in CR. Having insisted on this reality, it then becomes imperative for researchers to identify those structures that generate those social events and discourses. These structures are not irreducible to some observable patterns of events and discourses and are therefore not spontaneously apparent[3]. They comprise of human relations (or rules and practices governing such relations) connecting actors, and/or the material artifacts like technology systems, both associated with the phenomenon of interest[4]. They can only be identified through practical and theoretical work of the social sciences through empirically controlled investigations. Identifying these generative structures will not only help us understand the social world better but equip us to change or transform it, explaining the critical in CR.

According to CR, the existence of real and intransitive social structures is a necessary condition for any intentional human activity – they preexist any human action. But these social structures do not exist independently of human volition. All social structures that we encounter, whether in a family, community, nation, at school, at work, or at leisure depend upon, and presuppose social relations (between the father and son, the teacher and pupil, the player and the captain, and between the team-member and the team-manager) into which we all enter. Through our everyday activities, we enter into these preexisting structures and intentionally or unintentionally reproduce and/or transform them. This position allows CR to avoid the pitfalls of both, voluntarism and structuralism-voluntarism that stresses on the agentic action and atomistic individualism, and structuralism that makes humans a puppet in the hands of reified, collective social structures. CR views the social to be essentially *relational*, consisting of and depending on social relations. Society is thus seen to be an ensemble of positioned practices and networked inter-relationships which individuals never create, but presuppose and in doing so, transform or reproduce them. While social structures are dependent on the consciousness of agents who reproduce or transform them, they cannot be reduced to this consciousness. They always have a material or a real dimension. This relational view implies that a person's individuality is constituted by his or her social particularity. In other words, we are mainly a product of what we do, and what has been done to us in particular social relations in which we were born, and in which we work, play, and live. Methodological individualism is eschewed here because facts about society and social phenomena cannot be explained solely in terms of facts about individuals. But neither can individual behavior be mechanistically described in terms of the social structures in which they work, play, and live. These structures do not exist as collective molds into which the individual is merely fitted, thereby also eschewing collectivism. CR sees society as both the condition and outcome of human agency and human agency can both reproduce and transform society. The paradigm here is that of a sculptor at work fashioning a product out of the material and with the tools available to him or her. CR sees people in their social activity performing a double function: they not only make social products but make the conditions of their making, that is, reproduce (or transform) the structures governing their activities of production. Agency, thus, relates more to human intentionality. It stems from the fact that persons are material things with a degree of neurophysiological complexity that enables them not just, like the higher animals, to initiate changes in a purposeful way, to monitor and control their performances, but to monitor the monitoring of these performances and comment on them[5]. However, there is an important asymmetry here: at any moment of time, society is pre-given for individuals who never create it, but merely reproduce or transform it[6]. The social world is always pre-structured. Agents are acting in a world of structural constraints and possibilities they did not produce. The rules of linguistics and grammar, like natural structures, impose limits upon the speech acts that we perform, but they do not determine our performances. Or, people do not marry to produce a family, but it is the unintended consequence and an inexorable result of, and as much a necessary condition for, this activity. Social structure then is both the ever-present condition and continually reproduced outcome of intentional human agency.

Given that our knowledge of social reality is historically, socially, and culturally situated: it is context, concept, and activity-dependent, and it can be articulated from varying standpoints and using diverse ways. Therefore, our knowledge will always be perspectival, finite, contextual, and fallible, entailing a methodological pluralism that comes from embracing what the CR calls as *epistemic relativism*. Knowledge is dependent on the knower and is created by the knower, and can thus change from knower to knower. Actors' accounts are both corrigible and limited by the existence of unacknowledged conditions, unintended consequences, tacit skills, and unconscious motivations. But they do form the indispensable starting point of any social inquiry. This pluralism entails that we respect all views and be open to other views. Realism calls for an unsparing commitment to truth but also recognizes that there is no truth outside of historical time. Therefore, all our representations and perspectives will have limitations, and our ways of knowing this truth (epistemology) will only be done under more or less historically transient conditions. According to Bhaskar, the enterprise to know about the world is transitive. All methods, arrays, and techniques (grounded in our epistemology) are human dependent and inherently social and historical. And he has gone on a lot to say about our endemic nonrecognition of this fallibility[7]. It has led to what he calls the *epistemic fallacy*, our absolute identification of our belief about what is (ontology) to what/how we can know about it (epistemology). Epistemic fallacy is the naïve reduction of ontology to epistemology, where we conflate the reality to our knowledge of reality.

For the critical realists, the social world is not closed like the natural world, but much like the natural world, it is structured, differentiated, and hierarchical. It is multi-determined, multi-leveled, multi-linear, and multi-perspectival, with higher-order agencies setting the boundary conditions for lower-order laws. This stratification is in the form of mechanisms (associated with structures), the events they generate, and the subset of events that are actually experienced. These are the domains of the **Real,** the **Actual,** and the **Empirical**. The real contains the whole of reality – mechanisms, events, and experiences. The actual consists of events that occur, spurred by the generative mechanisms in the real. Out of these, the subset of events that are experienced by human senses forms the empirical. We cannot reduce all events to those that are observed, and we cannot reduce enduring causal mechanisms to the observed regularities.

We conclude this section by alluding to another key tenet of CR, that of *judgmental rationality*. It accounts for the fact that since we are realists in our ontologies, and relativists with regard to our epistemology, we must formulate criteria for judging which accounts about the world hold good to us, and provide a plausible explanation of our social inquiry. It is imperative that we take the responsibility of making this evaluation about the diverse and competing claims about the world, and be able to offer objective reasons for affirming one view over the others.

And lastly, true to its credo, CR does not lay down any specific research methodology and technique/tool that should govern a research endeavor. We will go on to show how our chosen methodology of work ethnographies in organizations allowed us to seamlessly weave in the theoretical underpinnings of CR in the practical 'under-laboring' of our research work. It guided us from field-note taking to analyzing the data, to making connections with what was happening outside of these organizations, and helped us arrive at concrete explanations of the phenomena we wished to understand.

A.1.1 Principles of critical realism embedded in our work ethnography

As we saw above, CR has a series of philosophical positions on a range of matters, and there is a broad pool of key tenets and positions from which critical realists draw upon[8]. For our work ethnography, we relied primarily on the following key principles:

Duality of Structure and Agency without a reductionist collapse in either direction. We relied on the works of Roy Bhasker and Margaret Archer to look at social phenomenon within the organization we studied, through the lens of both, structure and agency, but taking care to analytically separate the two while illustrating such phenomena. This ontology premises that the social world (like the natural world) has a plurality of structures, which can be identified and which are independent of our perception, but these structures (unlike the natural world) presuppose social relations into which we enter. Social structures are dependent on the consciousness of agents who can reproduce (or transform) them, but they cannot be reduced to this consciousness. We paraphrase again, the ontological basis of our research.

> *Structures depend on the enduring relations, which agents enter into (that pre-exist them), but these structures can be (and are) transformed or reproduced by human agents, either intentionally or unconsciously.*

Our ethnography in the IT services organization revolved crucially around one key aspect – what do we observe during our ethnographic work? CR's duality of structure and agency gave us our answer. It led us to focus first on the structural aspects of the organizations that we studied, and then on the agentic aspects associated with participants within these organizations. It was the peg around which we decided to weave all our ethnographic field reports.

The three nested domains of Reality. Social phenomena are the products of a plurality of structures and these may be hierarchically ranked in terms of their explanatory importance. CR begins by talking of a domain of events that are independent of our perceptions of them (what Bhaskar calls an intransitive real). And, indeed, these events would exist whether or not they were observed or there even were observers. Nested within this intransitive real is a domain of actual events, only a (small) subset of which are perceived and become empirical experiences. The domain of the events is in the Actual (all events that have happened), while the domain of the experience is in the empirical (that we observe). Perception is significant because not all events are empirical. Regular sequences of events are not laws. These are mere conditions. There is something else that causes, which is present in the domain of the Real, which has to be adduced by the researchers. So very early on, we were cognizant of the fact that for understanding the two key observations in our ethnography (i) surge of AI-related projects in the Indian IT services organizations and (ii) the hurdles faced by the engineers with a non–IT background in these projects, we had to go beyond the obvious explanations couched in the specific nature of the IT organization or its organizational practices. For teasing out the generative mechanisms, we had to look at some aspects of the Real that actualized these and allowed them to happen (Actual). Figure A.1 summarizes these relations.

A retroductive, applied science methodology. The aim of a retroductive research strategy is to discover underlying causal mechanisms that, in particular contexts, explain observed regularities[9]. A retroductive strategy about any observed social phenomenon would involve asking questions about why those phenomena are being observed, going beyond mere description of them. Apriori assumptions are kept weak, and field methods are strengthened to gain all possible knowledge about the phenomena. Going with

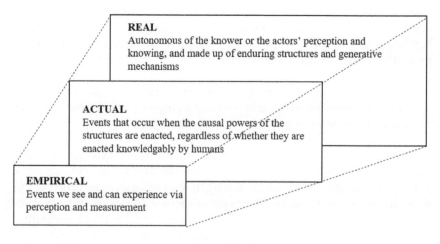

Figure A.1 Nested real, actual, and empirical in CR

this ignorance about the causal mechanisms at work, retroducing involves unearthing these mechanisms based on prior knowledge or existing theories from other areas of study[10]. CR specifically refrains from advocating a particular approach to data collection to which researchers should subscribe. Retroduction therefore should be understood as a framework by which researchers analyze findings; a framework by which one attempts to identify causal mechanisms[11]. The retroductive model categorizes knowledge into the three nested categories we described above of the Empirical, the Actual, and the Real. In qualitative research, this would involve[12]:

- The Empirical: refers to taking of notes of interactive messages that are conveyed in the time spent with the research participants.
- The Actual: the process of analysis when the researcher perceives the connections.
- The Real: the researchers gleaning out the mechanisms and structures accounting for these connections and relationships between categories.

In the IT industry that we were studying, unlike say other social structures like economy or religion, it was not difficult to look at technology underlying the real/intransitive structures. That also explains the ease with which IS researchers have taken to CR as a meta-theoretical frame[13]. But in recognizing fallibility of the observed events, the researcher recognizes that an actor's accounts are limited by unintended consequences, unacknowledged conditions, unconscious motivations, and tacit skills, all of which are a part of the Real that is not empirically observed (in ethnographies) or even talked about in conversations (however impromptu) and interviews. These could only be teased out through an epistemology involving a continual process of empirically controlled retroduction of explanatory structures from the manifest phenomenon produced by them. We had to follow the basic schema of applied scientific explanation outlined in CR research[14]. The first step is the description of the concrete observable phenomenon. The next step is to retroduce possible explanations, which would call for the elimination of what will always constitute a plurality of causes in open systems until one has identified a full enough set of causes for a concrete applied explanation. The last step involves redescribing the initial phenomenon in the light of the causal mechanisms at work.

A.1.2 Work ethnography

The objective of our research was to understand and depict the role of the IT industry in characterizing the mobility seen in India, post 2000, especially for Indian engineers. During the early stages of our research, we explored all available secondary data sources and their survey instruments around employment and unemployment, and surveyed existing methods that would help us identify the patterns of social or occupational mobility in the country. We found that in the Indian context, there was insufficient data to analyze occupational mobility in the country in general, let alone studying mobility specifically in the context of the Indian IT industry. This lack of secondary data meant that we had to rely on conducting primary research through case studies or field surveys or ethnography, to get answers. We felt that the complexity of social mobility as a phenomenon made the case study method a difficult choice, since this would require multiple case studies covering sufficient variety and complexity concerning the IT industry and the educational backgrounds of engineers working in this industry. Questionnaire-based primary surveys targeting engineers or prospective engineers in the Indian IT industry were ruled out because of the sheer paucity of relevant information. Our research required a grounds–up explanatory analysis of what is driving this mobility rather than formulating tentative hypotheses around this issue and testing them through survey instruments. Ethnography, therefore, was our preferred choice. For us, ethnography meant embedding within research contexts as participant observers. Accordingly, in an IT services organization, the ethnographer worked as a full-time intern within an AI research unit working on ongoing AI projects with other team members. As a precursor to this primary study, the ethnographer also conducted participant-observation-based ethnography by working as a data analytics tutor in a nonautonomous engineering college. The *emic* accounts of the ethnographer focused mainly on the structural and agentic aspects of the said organizations. The *etic* required situating these organizations within the broader historical and policy context. In order to do this, existing journal articles, published reports, and pertinent newspaper articles that discussed the historical and policy contexts surrounding our ethnographic sites were studied. A key finding that we came across in the field, driven primarily by our open-ended ethnographic methodology, was the significant influence of emerging technologies, particularly AI, in these two research contexts. This therefore led us to focus much more on this specific structural (technological) aspect within these contexts, particularly with regard to the IT services organization.

Our research methodology was also motivated by the works of Barley & Kunda (2001), who propose the use of ethnography research and its capacity to reveal not only the 'native point of view' (emic) but also the 'analytical constructs that are removed from the native point of view' (etic) as a way of 'bringing work back into organizations.'[15] According to them, adopting methods such as ethnography at a workplace that can yield detailed descriptions of work-life within an organization allowing researchers to systematically investigate the concrete activities constituting work practices and processes within it. Research on work practices emphasizes 'moment by moment flow of activity', interactions over attributes and structures and enables researchers to focus on the dynamics of organizing, detailing the situated (in situ) 'integration of tools, documents, action, and interaction.'[16] Workplace ethnographies, according to them, allow for a more nuanced understanding of organizational change by bringing complexities of work into the foreground, in comparison to other methods which simply gloss over such work complexities. Another motivation for adopting ethnography as our method is driven by the works of Burawoy et al. (2000), who call for conducting 'global ethnography', which is a 'historically grounded, theoretically driven, macro ethnography.'[17] In the context of our study, this not only pushed us to inquire about the work practices and processes in-situ within these empirical settings, but it also motivated us to constantly relate it with the extant historical and theoretical underpinnings about the work that was being carried out in similar settings within their respective organizational fields. Therefore, our objective was to get a macro-level understanding of the changes happening within the Indian IT industry and engineering education landscape in the times of emerging technologies (which is etic) by looking through the lens of these two organizations (which is emic). The etic perspectives were the responsibility of the research team as a whole, which were discussed regularly and helped bolster the emic ethnography field notes. This constant to and fro between the etic and emic also enabled a more focused gathering and structuring of the field notes in an ongoing fashion.

CR's philosophical underpinnings and its theoretical clarity on the Structure-Agency elision[18] call for a need to 'analytically differentiate' structure and agency, especially in situations where the two are seen as inseparable and therefore often conflated. Very early on, therefore, in our ethnography, this prodded us to deliberately investigate autonomous features, pertaining either to structure or agency. The premises of CR indeed were crucial to our ethnography in helping us retroduce the generative structures of the Indian IT organizations that influence the agency of individuals in the kind of skills they transpose while working on AI projects. This allowed us to illustrate the role played by organizational structures in enabling/constraining the potential of individuals in their efforts at transposing their prior skillsets, their efforts at transforming them and/or their intentional or unintentional reproduction of those very structures.

A.2 Critical realism and ethnography findings

In Chapters 3 and 4, we laid out our broad research findings a-theoretically. In this section, we elaborate on how the key tenets of CR we charted above helped unearth these findings – preventing our getting lost in the minutiae of daily field notes. Two key features of CR were a bulwark to our analyses (a) Duality of Structure and Agency (b) The three-hierarchical domains of the Real, the Actual, and the Empirical that we had to tease out through retroduction. Below, we elaborate on the role played by each.

A.2.1 Separation of structure and agency

The analytical separation of Structure and Agency was the peg around which we wrote our field notes. Structures refer to the 'given' objects on which conscious human activity takes place. This 'given' could be material or ideational. In this particular work ethnography in the AI research lab, the real structures could be numerous: the IT industry in India, the specific ITeS organization within it, the AI research lab situated within this organization, projects that it undertakes, and the technologies which determines its workflows. The ideational structures could be the skills (tacit and explicit) that the engineers come with, the expectations of the managers, the clients, and the organization. Because social structures are ultimately social products, they are possible objects of transformation and can only be relatively enduring. And because social activities are interdependent, social structures can be only relatively autonomous. Society can thus be conceived as an ensemble of such relatively enduring and independent structures and they do not exist independently of the conception of their agents. Agency would refer primarily to the acts and intentions of the various actors in the lab that we had to identify – those of the data engineers, the data scientists, the cloud and software engineers, the business analysts, the project managers, and the team lead.

The importance of distinguishing between structure and agency is now apparent – since the two possess very different properties. Rules of grammar in a language, for example, pose limits on our speech, but they do not determine our performance. However, the way people use language does unconsciously reproduce or transform language and its rules. So, people in their conscious human activity unconsciously reproduce (or occasionally transform) the social structures that govern their substantive activities of production.

The sharp distinction between structure and agency allowed us to study how agents differing in their backgrounds read or perceive organizational structures differently and thereby chart their own mobility pathways. This analytical separation of structure and agency also allows us to explain the differences in the way different actors actualize organizational structures, which in turn might enable or constrain their mobility chances. This need to 'analytically differentiate' structure and agency[19], especially in situations where the two are seen as inseparable and therefore often conflated, was at the very heart of our ethnographic field notes. Very early on in our ethnography, this prodded us to deliberately investigate autonomous features, pertaining either to structure or agency. Our ethnographic observations revealed the dominant structures at play that largely influenced the agency of individuals in terms of the skills they are expected to transpose during projects. This allowed us to illustrate the role played by organizational structures in enabling/limiting the potential of individuals in these efforts, which was critical for understanding their mobility prospects within this organization.

We illustrate this analytical division in the Table A.1 through the coding process of our field notes. This process allowed us to infer that the AI projects undertaken by this lab were conscious acts (of business analysts, project managers, and the team lead, among others) of engaging with their existing software clients to take care of their digital transformation needs. The clients also found it easier to negotiate with an organization that had a proven track record in delivering their IT-related outsourced services. The workflows negotiated, therefore, fell within the known rubric of their existing software projects. This was the organizational structure within which everybody in this research lab willy-nilly

Table A.1 Coding our field notes – an example

Sample Paragraph from Field notes: *"The senior most software architect said that challenges to career progression or mobility will depend on the organization and individual mentality. The organization and team you work for matters. There is difference between service-based companies – the major recruiters in India, and the product-based companies. Product-based organizations can afford to have long-term commitments because they are delivering a product rather than providing service. Service-based companies are involved in maintaining, updating and developing the software depending upon the requirement of clients. This is very different from building generic products that are purchased by a diverse set of clients. Service-based companies run on a safer bet because you are not developing products but only providing services. As a result, when compared to product-based companies which have to spend heavily on marketing their products and increasing brand value, for service-based companies the need to spend time and efforts in marketing is relatively less. Workflows in product-based companies are not as stringent as in service-based companies. This gives employees greater freedom to hone their skills to some extent in the way they want. I believe product-based companies give greater mobility prospects than the service-based companies mainly because of the stringent workflows observed in case of the latter. Individual mentality also matters in the context of mobility. Especially for new joinees posted in a team, I think it is their individual responsibility to improve their skills both horizontally and vertically. By horizontally, they should have some idea about what the other teams to do. More understanding the better. By vertically, they should work toward building expertise at the work in their own team. For example, I am expert in Cloud, but I also know Java, I can work on AI/ML flows, I know about many other IT-related stuff broadly. This is because in each team I worked I not only built my skills there but also expanded my skills that other peripheral teams also were doing. This gives me confidence. For example, whenever market for cloud is down, I can go back to Java or vice versa. If one fails to spend time on improving skills in this way, there is a chance that he/she will remain like a frog in a well. In this industry, employees also have to take the responsibility for their survival. The ideal thing to do is instead of dedicating yourself to your company, dedicate yourself to the work that you do. In our industry, switching across companies is inevitable. Therefore, you also need a group of friends who can support you and on whom you can rely upon. These people may also refer you when they go to work in other good companies. Whether this company or other, your skills and the people around you matter the most in terms of your job prospects."* Paraphrased from discussion with a senior software architect

Coding and summarization-in-brief, done by the mentor to guide the ethnographer's observations during subsequent visits:

		Emic perspective	Etic perspective	Questions/Pointers
Structure	**Technological aspects**	Gaining technical expertise in the tools used by one's own team, and a decent understanding about the work done by peripheral teams is crucial for mobility.	There is a preference toward clear division of work between roles. But having expertise beyond one's own work is crucial for employees to move up the career ladder.	Does the nature of work division between individuals vary by the technology (like software or AI or IoT)?

(Continued)

Table A.1 Coding our field notes – an example (*Continued*)

		Emic perspective	Etic perspective	Questions/Pointers
	Organizational aspects	There is a difference between service-based and product-based companies. Service-based companies are relatively more client-centric.	Service-based companies have relatively rigid workflows when compared to product-based companies.	Do greater client-centricity affect the nature of workflows in service-based organizations?
Agency	**Participants' viewpoint**	Employees should build skills horizontally and vertically, and build trust-based relationships with their peers.	Switching between companies is common in the IT industry and both the skills and the networks determine the nature of employee job switches.	Is there a relationship between service-based organizational work and the prevalence of switching between companies?

ended up working. It resulted in two things (unconsciously or unintentionally): (a) Most of the AI projects undertaken by this lab ended up being at the lower end of the clients' value chain, where the output can be billed and delivered per the metrics of their software services. These were the 'augmented' AI services that they bundled along with their traditional software services, which did not score high on the AI value chain as well. Most of the activities higher up the AI value chain were done independently by the data scientists more as a research activity. (b) This also explained the persistence of the IT/non-IT divide in the workforce, where the non-IT data engineers found it very difficult to meaningfully engage in these projects. They were working under structures unsuited to the tools or skills for which they were recruited. In beginner roles and fairly junior, they ended up trying to reproduce these structures rather than actively trying to transform them. The transformation of structures more suited to the AI workflows could only have been attempted by the senior data scientists in the lab, who had taken tentative steps in that direction.

A.2.2 *Retroducing the hierarchical domains of the real, actual, and empirical*

We were able to retroduce these findings because CR begins with the premise that reality is autonomous of the knower or the actors' perception and knowing – *ontological realism*. In this intransitive real, lie the enduring structures and generative mechanisms underlying and producing observable phenomena and events[20] that have been unearthed through meticulous research. Social reality is not only real but stratified. Structures possess ontological depth, that is, their existence lies behind, and affects the manifest phenomena[21]. Critical realist approach proposes a triune stratification, the intransigent Real (the whole of the intransitive reality – structures with their causal mechanisms inherent to them), the Actual (the events that occur when the causal powers of the structures are enacted, regardless of whether they are enacted knowledgeably by humans) and the Empirical (those events we see and can experience via perception and measurement). This stratification is in the forms of three nested domains: the intransitive structures with their causal mechanisms, the events they generate, and the subset of events that are actually experienced – the domains of the Real, the Actual, and the Empirical. Perception is significant because not all events are empirical. In the following paragraph, following the work of Wynn and Williams[22], we look at what each of these domains constitutes.

The real domain is constituted by structures which bear mechanisms that are 'ways of acting of things', inherent to physical objects or social structures. Such mechanisms are understood as causal powers or tendencies of structures. The individual actors and components of structures are assumed to bear causal powers based on their thoughts and beliefs of how given actions are linked to consequences. But not all causal mechanisms can be attributable to human actors. Particularly in IS research settings, apart from social structures and physical objects, technological artifacts could be the source of emergent powers, which along with the actors' beliefs could generate causal mechanisms that need to be examined. The actual domain includes specific happenings or events, resulting from the activation of causal tendencies emanating from structures of the real layer, which may or may not be perceived. Multitude of events could have been generated, but not all their effects can be perceived or discerned. This is especially true of complex events which are less likely to directly perceive. The empirical domain is made up of experiences or those events which we can directly observe through sensory perceptions or sensory enhancing tools. CR therefore recognizes that experiences of the empirical are only a subset of the actual events generated in a given context.

In this study, this hierarchical, nested stratification allowed us to tease out the generative mechanisms of the phenomena we were observing/studying. What was most obvious to the ethnographer in the NLP project working with colleagues, the various observations and conversations with team members was (a) the peculiar 'augmented' nature of the AI projects taken up by this lab, described above, and (b) the inordinate amount of effort and time spent by the data engineers in programming-related tasks. This fell squarely within the domain of the **empirical**/the observable – that which was apparent to the ethnographer. It was what got reflected most in the memory markers and field notes of the ethnographer. In the weekly meeting with the research mentor, what had to be consciously done was to go behind/beyond the obvious (the fact that Indian IT organizations are still to catch up with the global technology giants in AI projects or the poor training in programming in the non-IT engineering streams) and situate these in the Actual and the Real structures.

The **Real** in this case was made up of two interrelated structural aspects. The first of them is the rationale that the senior managerial roles of this unit carry with regard to these AI-augmented projects. Such projects prevent this unit from becoming a cost center in this highly competitive space in which most Indian IT organizations operate. The second aspect is related to the dominance of software engineering practices while implementing AI projects, often contrary to the principles of ideal AI project workflows.

As per the practices that got actualized, coordination between data engineers and between cloud or software engineers relied on high-level frameworks or plans devised by business analysts and cloud architects for these projects. These were unsuited to ideal-typical AI projects that are centered around a use-case and the corresponding data, and the ML model choices, given this data. Because of the clients' concerns related to data sharing and model interpretability, the augmented projects undertaken by this team tend to become less centered around data and consequently also distanced from the use-case. These were the unacknowledged conditions around which the members of this research lab ended up working. This was in the realm of the **actual**. So, while these were data-related projects, their augmented nature made them less data-centric. Data-centric and use-case optimal solution enhancement opportunities only arose post-deployment when full data of client got fed into their preprocessing programs through secure user interfaces. The unease of the data engineers was a reaction to this realized event. They found that they could not transpose their tacit domain skills, but were caught up in programming tasks related to the cleaning and structuring of the clients' (limited) data. This was led by the unconscious motivation of the team lead and managers to have them take on the easily divisible, allocable, and thereby the easily billable tasks.

Data, in most such AI projects, is not only closely related to the client's specific domain and business understanding but also drives the appropriate choice of ML models. This requires a theoretical understanding of statistics or machine learning. The data engineers believed that given their industrial engineering background, they had the required skills around both these. But their expectations were thwarted when faced with the daunting burden of software engineering practices being followed in these projects. They only had a working knowledge of programming and were mainly recruited for their domain knowledge – statistics and industrial engineering education. Getting caught up in the programming-related work that the project manager and business analyst assigned to them was the unintended consequence of the structures at work in the real domain. These aspects of the structures in this lab were the ones that were actualized, thanks to the importance given by the senior managerial roles to customization, reuse, and clear task allocation, over iterative experimentation and building use-case optimal solutions from scratch. Cost concerns, showcasing incremental status updates to clients, and incompatible project workflows are some key drivers for such preponderance of software engineering practices in AI projects. This doesn't alter the work environment for cloud and software engineers working on AI projects. Their mobility pathways get decided by the expertise they gain in technical aspects related to software development in the era of cloud, and less around statistical knowledge or business understanding.

The data scientists in this lab are making efforts to build AI-compatible workflows centered around data, meant to facilitate iterative experimentation between different activities – preprocessing, model building, and deployment. Even here, our ethnographic findings show that only those junior data scientists (previously data engineers) who had programming backgrounds were chosen. Since building these workflow enhancements also required programming expertise in addition to theoretical understanding of statistics and machine learning. This again points to the importance of programming background – on top of statistics or domain knowledge – for data engineers to move up their career ladder. Therefore, for data engineers from non-IT backgrounds, we see that their prior educational background is indeed an important factor impeding their mobility prospects within a **real**, domain consisting of structures jointly influenced by technologies, and the beliefs and expectations set by the senior technical and managerial roles. The data engineers were caught up in the **empirical**, consisting of work practices – which were to undertake data preprocessing work mainly related to programming. The events they perceive are closer to aspects of software engineering, and not so much around the intricacies of work expected in ideal-typical AI projects. The ML workflows being developed in this unit, which are meant to shift the focus from programming expertise to the more ideal AI project workflows are in the **actual** but not yet perceivable to these data engineers. Also, actualizing such workflows is inherently a challenging task as it will require deliberations with clients who currently find the traditional software workflows convenient. Figure A.2 depicts the stratification of activities along empirical, actual, and real layers.

Gleaning these explanatory mechanisms also called for an epistemology involving a continual process of retroduction of the not-so-obvious structures from the obvious and apparent phenomenon produced by them. It was here that ethnography, as a method of social science research, gave us tremendous advantage. The regular discussions within the research team based on the daily field notes of the ethnographer were at the heart of this process. A key CR tenet underlined the discussions during these weekly meetings of the research team: that an actor's accounts are always limited by unintended consequences, unacknowledged conditions, unconscious motivations, and tacit skills, all of which are a part of the Real that is not empirically observed. These may not be able immediately accessible to the ethnographer through observations or conversations with team members.

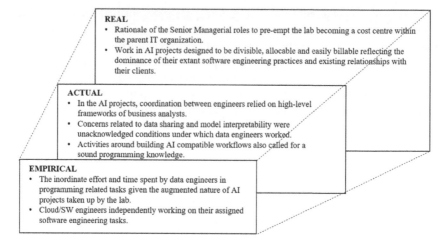

REAL
- Rationale of the Senior Managerial roles to pre-empt the lab becoming a cost centre within the parent IT organization.
- Work in AI projects designed to be divisible, allocable and easily billable reflecting the dominance of their extant software engineering practices and existing relationships with their clients.

ACTUAL
- In the AI projects, coordination between engineers relied on high-level frameworks of business analysts.
- Concerns related to data sharing and model interpretability were unacknowledged conditions under which data engineers worked.
- Activities around building AI compatible workflows also called for a sound programming knowledge.

EMPIRICAL
- The inordinate effort and time spent by data engineers in programming related tasks given the augmented nature of AI projects taken up by the lab.
- Cloud/SW engineers independently working on their assigned software engineering tasks.

Figure A.2 Stratification of activities along empirical–actual–real

They have to be teased out through retroduction, following CR's stratificatory schema of the social world.

We hope we have been able to illustrate and explicate the usefulness of this reflexive mode of science through our work ethnography. It was necessary for us to first identify the concrete, observable phenomena in this AI research lab. The theoretical frames of CR dictated our field notes. Having located the empirical observations within a specific AI project, for retroducing back to its antecedent causes we had to trace it to its extra-local and often unobservable determinations. Since ethnography does not stop at its tracks but has to necessarily incorporate the wider context through a constant back and forth between the etic and the emic, we were in a good position to carry out these retroductions.

A.2.3 Some reflections on our work ethnography

The context and the narratives from the field forming the basis of our ethnography are very different from positivist methodologies stressing the three Rs: Reliability, Replicability, and Representativeness. For Reliability and Replicability, the more positivist methods believe in having a fixed framework through which to extract information (interview schedules, structured/semi-structured questionnaires). We believe that in ethnographic studies, one ought to not have such a predefined template, because one could begin with one set of questions but end with different ones. Revisiting our ethnographies in this regard, we did go to the field with a set of presuppositions, questions, and frameworks – but they were more like prisms rather than frameworks – more emergent than fixed. In our case, our presupposition was that the IT industry in India is playing and will continue to play a key role in India's mobility story. This had to be our primary site of research in order to understand this phenomenon. Embedded in the field, we realized that this industry was itself undergoing a flux, thanks to the entry of emerging technologies like AI. The pandemic, we realized, was normalizing a lot of work procedures like work from home that were hitherto being done sporadically. Had we stuck to a predefined framework of questionnaires, we would have missed these developments. This reflexive mode of scientific research, also propounded by CR, realizes that every piece of knowledge is situational – located in a specific time and space. The only way one can have representativeness and reliability is by painstakingly integrating situational knowledge into a social process. Multiple readings, multiple theoretical frames, and relevant cognate ethnographies help in such aggregation of a single ethnography into social processes. Having our broad research question in mind, we picked on the opportunity to participate in such a cognate ethnography in an Engineering College, which is the primary recruitment ground for this industry. Linking the aspirations of these Engineering students with the developments in the IT industry enriched our perspective. Because we were open and had the participant researchers' outlook, we could move with our participants in their space and time and produce situational knowledge, which was both discursive as well as nondiscursive. While the discursive knowledge emerged through narratives, the nondiscursive (un-explicated, unacknowledged, and tacit knowledge) had to be teased out retroductively through emic participation and etic analysis – by doing things with those whom we were studying. This unique insider/outsider perspective of our study allowed us to curate multiple readings from our ethnographies and aggregate them into the phenomena we were interested in studying.

Notes

1 http://www.asatheory.org/current-newsletter-online/what-is-critical-realism
2 https://en.wikipedia.org/wiki/Roy_Bhaskar
3 Bhaskar, R. (2010). Reclaiming reality: A critical introduction to contemporary philosophy. Taylor & Francis Group.
4 Wynn Jr, D. E., & Williams, C. K. (2020). Recent advances and opportunities for improving critical realism-based case study research in IS. Journal of the Association for Information Systems, 21(1), 8.
5 Bhaskar, R., (2008). Dialectic: The pulse of freedom. Routledge.
6 Archer, M., Bhaskar, R., Collier, A., Lawson, T., & Norrie, A. (Eds.). (1998). Critical realism: Essential readings. Routledge.
7 Bhaskar, R. (2010). Reclaiming reality: A critical introduction to contemporary philosophy. Taylor & Francis Group.
8 http://www.asatheory.org/current-newsletter-online/what-is-critical-realism
9 Bhaskar, R. (1975). A Realist Theory of Science. Leeds, Leeds Books. (Also republished 1989 and 1998; also excerpted in Archer, M., et al., (eds) (1998).
10 Wynn, D. E. & Williams, C. K. (2012). Principles for conducting critical realist case study research in information systems. MIS Quarterly, 36(3), 787–810.
11 Elder-Vass D. (2007). A method for social ontology. Journal of Critical Realism, 6(2), 226–249.

12 Bunt, S., 2018. Critical realism and grounded theory: Analysing the adoption outcomes for disabled children using the retroduction framework. Qualitative Social Work, 17(2), 176–194.

13 Wynn Jr, D. E., & Williams, C. K. (2020). Recent advances and opportunities for improving critical realism-based case study research in IS. Journal of the Association for Information Systems, 21(1), 8.

14 Bhaskar, R., 2008. *Dialectic: The pulse of freedom.* Routledge.

15 Barley, S. R., & Kunda, G. (2001). Bringing work back in. Organization Science, 12(1), 76–95.

16 Barley, S. R., & Kunda, G. (2001). Bringing work back in. Organization Science, 12(1), 76–95.

17 Burawoy, M., Blum, J. A., George, S., Gille, Z., & Thayer, M. (2000). Global ethnography: Forces, connections, and imaginations in a postmodern world. University of California Press. (p. 24).

18 Archer, M., Bhaskar, R., Collier, A., Lawson, T., & Norrie, A. (2013). Critical realism: Essential readings. Routledge.

19 Archer, M., Bhaskar, R., Collier, A., Lawson, T., & Norrie, A. (2013). Critical realism: Essential readings. Routledge.

20 Archer, M., Bhaskar, R., Collier, A., Lawson, T., & Norrie, A. (2013). Critical realism: Essential readings. Routledge.

21 Bhaskar, R. (2010). Reclaiming reality: A critical introduction to contemporary philosophy. Taylor & Francis Group.

22 Wynn Jr, D. E., & Williams, C. K. (2020). Recent advances and opportunities for improving critical realism-based case study research in IS. Journal of the Association for Information Systems, 21(1), 8.

Further readings

While our study relied on several articles, reports, books, papers, etc., from the current literature, some of them were particularly important as they helped us in giving a proper structure to our arguments and our reasoning. We listed down some of these articles within two sets. The first set of articles guided us with rich information about the growth and evolution trajectory of the Indian IT sector and the importance of engineers as a dominant workforce within this sector. The second set of articles provided us the necessary technological wherewithal to talk about the challenges that the Indian IT sector faced as it transitions toward emerging technologies.

1 The following articles provide rich contextual information about the Indian Information Technology sector and its workforce. Articles by Arora et al. (2001) and Jalote and Natarajan (2019) discuss the growth and evolution of the Indian IT sector in the past four decades. They cover the sector's journey from offering relatively low-end, cost-arbitrage, based services to more advanced services in recent times. Articles by Athreye (2005) and Dossani and Kenney (2007) highlight the relevance of offshore work taken up by the Indian IT sector globally, and the importance of its workforce in making it an attractive offshore destination for the clients. The book by Upadhya and Vasavi (2012) talks about the offshore work and workers in much greater detail from a sociological perspective. Articles by Herbsleb and Mockus (2003) and Ramasubbu et al. (2008) highlight the nature of work dispersion under standard work processes in the context of global offshore software development. Works by Manning et al. (2011), Oza (2006), and Rajkumar and Mani (2001) talk about factors contributing to the longevity of client-vendor relationships in the context of IT offshore outsourcing, with a particular attention to the Indian IT service providers. Article by Arora et al. (2001) also talks about engineers as being the dominant workforce within the Indian IT industry. The report on engineering education by Banerjee and Muley (2007) depicts the scale at which India generates engineers every year contrasting with other developed and developing nations. Reports by Ministry of Human Resource and Development (MHRD), and All

India Council for Technical Education (AICTE) highlight the role of IT sector as a dominant employer of engineers, and also discuss some curriculum interventions for engineering education so as to increase the employability of Indian engineers. Book by Ramnath (2017) traces the trajectory of engineers as a profession in the Indian context from post-independence (after 1947) until recent times. While the Indian IT sector is a dominant services exporter in the country, a look into the growth trajectory of non-services sectors is an important contextual element characterizing India's growth story. Articles by Lamba and Subramanian (2020) and Basu and Maertens (2007) illuminate India's growth story over the past several decades by offering rich empirical evidence. Article by Balakrishnan (2006) discusses the role of policy in supporting a tremendous growth of IT sector in the country.

AICTE. (2018). Engineering education in India: Short- and medium-term perspectives. All India Council for Technical Education, Government of India.

Arora, A., Arunachalam, V. S., Asundi, J., & Fernandes, R. (2001). The Indian software services industry. Research Policy, 30(8), 1267–1287.

Athreye, S. S. (2005). The Indian software industry and its evolving service capability. Industrial and Corporate Change, 14(3), 393–418.

Balakrishnan, P. (2006). Benign neglect or strategic intent? Contested lineage of Indian software industry. Economic and Political Weekly, 41(36), (Sep. 9–15, 2006), 3865–3872.

Banerjee, R., & Muley, V. P. (2007). Engineering education in India. Report to energy systems engineering, IIT Bombay, Sponsored by Observer Research Foundation, September, 14.

Basu, K., & Maertens, A. (2007). The pattern and causes of economic growth in India. Oxford Review of Economic Policy, 23(2), 143–167.

Dossani, R., & Kenney, M. (2007). The next wave of globalization: Relocating service provision to India. World Development, 35(5), 772–791.

Herbsleb, J. D., & Mockus, A. (2003). An empirical study of speed and communication in globally distributed software development. IEEE Transactions on Software Engineering, 29(6), 481–494.

Jalote, P., & Natarajan, P. (2019). The growth and evolution of India's software industry. Communications of the ACM, 62(11), 64–69.

Lamba, R., & Subramanian, A. (2020). Dynamism with incommensurate development: The distinctive Indian model. Journal of Economic Perspectives, 34(1), 3–30.

Manning, S., Lewin, A. Y., & Schuerch, M. (2011). The stability of offshore outsourcing relationships. Management International Review, 51(3), 381–406.

MHRD. (2003). Revitalizing Technical Education—Report on the review committee on AICTE. Ministry of Human Resource Development, Government of India.

Oza, N. V. (2006). An empirical evaluation of client-vendor relationships in Indian software outsourcing companies. School of Computer Science.

Rajkumar, T. M., & Mani, R. V. S. (2001). Offshore software development. Information Systems Management, 18(2), 63–74.

Ramasubbu, N., Mithas, S., Krishnan, M. S., & Kemerer, C. F. (2008). Work dispersion, process-based learning, and offshore software development performance. MIS Quarterly, 32(2), Special Issue on Information Systems Offshoring (Jun., 2008), 437–458.

Ramnath, A. (2017). The birth of an Indian profession: Engineers, industry, and the state, 1900–47. Oxford University Press.

Upadhya, C., & Vasavi, A. R. (2012). In an outpost of the global economy: Work and workers in India's information technology industry. Routledge.

2   The following articles provide insights about the nature of digital transformation driven by emerging technologies across industries and help us draw some comparisons between software development and the development of emerging technology solutions. For example, articles by Dopico et al. (2016) and Lasi et al. (2014) discuss the characteristics of emerging-technology-driven digital transformation that is diffusing across many industry verticals today in the name of industry 4.0. Article by Xu et al. (2018) delves deeper into the role of some important technologies that contribute toward realizing an industry 4.0 system. A significant portion of the literature on digital transformation talks about it in the context of large enterprises. However, there are also articles that focus on building context-specific industry 4.0 solutions for small and medium sized enterprises. Mittal et al. (2018) is one such article that does a comprehensive analysis of the differentiating characteristics of small and large enterprises and recommends steps to take industry 4.0 closer to small and medium sized enterprises. To better contextualize the journey of the Indian IT sector toward emerging technologies, it is important to understand the emerging-technologies-specific challenges that this sector could face. A difference of work and work roles between solution development in the emerging technologies' context, and in the context of traditional software development, becomes a relevant comparison to gauge such challenges, as the Indian IT sector significantly positioned itself as a mature player in the context of the latter. Articles by Bilgeri et al (2019) and Bumblauskas et al. (2020) present illustrative case studies around building IoT- and Blockchain-based solutions in two different industrial settings. They discuss the context-specific factors that shape the development and deployment of these solutions. Their illustrations help to draw the peculiar challenges that service providers offering emerging technology solutions to different clients may have to overcome. Articles by Amershi et al. (2019) and Sculley et al. (2015) specifically focus on the differences between workflows of traditional software development and AI solution development. The article by Taddy (2019) articulates AI in terms of its defining technological elements and argues for the importance of domain structure to be a vital technological element and the driver of other two elements – the data and the machine learning

models. Within the first four chapters of the book by Ghezzi et al. (1991) the fundamental principles of software engineering are elicited in great detail. These principles also apply to the more recent advancements in software development work and workflows – for example in the context of software development in cloud and DevOps tools for realizing agile software development processes. The latter aspects and their similarities to traditional software development are covered by Cito et al. (2015) and Leite et al. (2019).

Amershi, S., Begel, A., Bird, C., DeLine, R., Gall, H., Kamar, E., … Zimmermann, T. (2019). Software engineering for machine learning: A case study. 2019 IEEE/ACM 41st International Conference on Software Engineering: Software Engineering in Practice (ICSE-SEIP), 291–300. IEEE.

Bilgeri, D., Gebauer, H., Fleisch, E., & Wortmann, F. (2019). Driving process innovation with IoT field data. MIS Quarterly Executive, 18, 191–207.

Bumblauskas, D., Mann, A., Dugan, B., & Rittmer, J. (2020). A blockchain use case in food distribution: Do you know where your food has been? International Journal of Information Management, 52, 102008.

Cito, J., Leitner, P., Fritz, T., & Gall, H. C. (2015). The making of cloud applications: An empirical study on software development for the cloud. Proceedings of the 2015 10th Joint Meeting on Foundations of Software Engineering, 393–403.

Dopico, M., Gómez, A., De la Fuente, D., García, N., Rosillo, R., & Puche, J. (2016). A vision of industry 4.0 from an artificial intelligence point of view. Proceedings on the International Conference on Artificial Intelligence (ICAI), 407.

Ghezzi, C., Jazayeri, M., & Mandrioli, D. (1991). Fundamentals of software engineering. Prentice-Hall, Inc.

Lasi, H., Fettke, P., Kemper, H.-G., Feld, T., & Hoffmann, M. (2014). Industry 4.0. Business & Information Systems Engineering, 6(4), 239–242.

Leite, L., Rocha, C., Kon, F., Milojicic, D., & Meirelles, P. (2019). A survey of DevOps concepts and challenges. ACM Computing Surveys (CSUR), 52(6), 1–35.

Mittal, S., Khan, M. A., Romero, D., & Wuest, T. (2018). A critical review of smart manufacturing & industry 4.0 maturity models: Implications for small and medium-sized enterprises (SMEs). Journal of Manufacturing Systems, 49, 194–214.

Sculley, D., Holt, G., Golovin, D., Davydov, E., Phillips, T., Ebner, D., Chaudhary, V., Young, M., Crespo, J.-F., & Dennison, D. (2015). Hidden technical debt in machine learning systems. Advances in Neural Information Processing Systems, Proceedings of the 28th International Conference on Neural Information Processing Systems - Volume 2, 2503–2511.

Taddy, M. (2019). The technological elements of artificial intelligence. University of Chicago Press.

Xu, H., Yu, W., Griffith, D., & Golmie, N. (2018). A survey on industrial internet of things: A cyber-physical systems perspective. IEEE Access, 6, 78238–78259.

Index

Note: Page number with *Italics* for the figures and **Bold** for the tables.